D0849037

The Supervisor and On-the-Job Training

Fourth Edition

MARTIN M. BROADWELL

ADDISON-WESLEY PUBLISHING

Reading, Massachusetts • Menlo Park, California

New York • Don Mills, Ontario • Wokingham, England

Amsterdam • Bonn • Sydney • Singapore • Tokyo • Madrid

San Juan • Paris • Seoul • Milan • Mexico City • Taipei

The publisher offers discounts on this book when ordered in quantity for special sales. For more information please contact:

Corporate & Professional Publishing Group
Addison-Wesley Publishing Company
One Jacob Way
Reading, Massachusetts 01867

Library of Congress Cataloging-in-Publication Data

Broadwell, Martin M.
　　　The supervisor and on-the-job training / Martin M. Broadwell. —
4th ed.
　　　　　p.　cm.
　　　Includes index.
　　　ISBN 0-201-56363-0
　　　1. Employees—Training of.　　I. Title.
HF5549.5.T7B72　　1995　　　　　　　　　　　　　　　　　　94-25336
658.3'1243—dc20　　　　　　　　　　　　　　　　　　　　　　　CIP

Typography by The Type Shoppe, Inc., Chestertown, Maryland

ISBN 0-201-56363-0

Text printed on recycled and acid-free paper.
1 2 3 4 5 6 7 8 9 10 CRW 97969594
First printing August 1994

Dedication

*To six grand grandchildren: Mason, Two Timothys,
Douglas, Daniel and Katie.*

*You've taught me a lot in my old age. Someday I hope
you'll be using this book to learn
the many things you need to know for adulthood.
But, more than that, I hope you'll be
writing your own books, perhaps on how to be
a better grandfather!*

CONTENTS

PREFACE TO THE FOURTH EDITION

What seems in one edition to be the "latest thing out" soon becomes out of date, or less than the full story. So it is with this book. It is rather amazing to the author that this creation has survived and the need for it has continued. It is also gratifying to know that supervisors and trainers continue to take on-the-job training (OJT) seriously. It is perhaps an understatement to point out that perhaps 95 percent of on-the-job training is done so poorly that the job performance suffers noticeably, and both the trainer and trainee usually agree it is the trainee's fault—which it isn't! The problem is simple: Most training is done simply by showing and telling, which seems logical enough. However, when looking at the chapter on "How to Do On-the-Job Training," one quickly sees the need for having the trainee do some telling and showing.

Some more progressive organizations are using a rather clever procedure to assure the best possible training of their trainees. They are giving "Train-the-Learner" training to those who are going to be trained. Essentially, they are telling the trainees how they should be trained, and suggesting that if the trainers don't use the suggested methods, then no record should be made that training has been done. This is quite effective for getting the trainers to follow proper procedures. To enhance both of these needs, Appendix B offers an outline for conducting either a "Train-the-Trainer" course or a "Train-the-Learner" course. They would be essentially the same.

Chapter 1, Why Train?, determines good and bad training, as well as good and bad reasons for training. It details the supervisor's responsibility for training, especially for new employees. The chapter also defines training to overcome deficiencies. Chapter 2, Why and How People Learn, examines human learning. People learn for many reasons, with three basic categories: desire for reward, fear of punishment, and curiosity. Good training tries to address all three of these motivators. There are reasons why people don't learn. The supervisor has to understand, recognize, and overcome these reasons. Chapter 3, On-the-Job Training or Classroom Training?, examines the similarities and distinct differences between the two methods. Good communications is common to both, as is the importance of the instructor–employee relationship. OJT is usually one-on-one, at the job location, making it more real and personal. OJT has other advantages, but some disadvantages, too, as the chapter reveals.

Chapter 4, Analyzing the Job to Be Done: I, shows that to analyze a job, we have to define a "good job" first. There are several reasons why employees don't perform, and lack of training is only one of them. Make sure training will help. Judge the value of training by watching previously trained people perform. Chapter 5, Analyzing the Job to Be Done: II, demonstrates several ways to break down the job: work analysis; job analysis; and work flow. The chapter uses charts for break down. It also shows how job description differs from job analysis, which is needed before training can take place. Chapter 6, Determining Objectives, discusses how objectives for training are the best way to design and measure training. The chapter shows how to write meaningful, doable, observable objectives, and examines the issue of accountability for success or failure of training. Chapter 7, Preparing to Train, is directed at the supervisors' tasks to prepare for employee training. It highlights potential problems, use of a supervisor's knowledge, preparation of an outline, and the proper timing and location for training.

Chapter 8, How to Do On-the-Job Training, looks in depth at actual OJT requirements and techniques. It includes self-preparation for supervisors, preparing the employee, building confidence, building interest, showing advantages to the employee, teaching beside the employee, stepping in when necessary during training, and using the same steps in classroom setting. Chapter 9, Special Considerations discusses new employee old job—advantages and disadvantages, and experienced employee new job—dealing with change. It also examines overcoming resistance to training and change. Chapter 10, What to Do When the Training Is Over, instructs how to evaluate and record the training. It discusses follow-up after training as the final key to success and the importance of immediate application of what was learned during training. Chapter 11, Training for Career Advancement, defines the problem and suggests that changing attitudes may be required. It emphasizes the great need for success and for a positive approach. Follow-up and evaluation are also covered.

It should be noted that the process of conducting OJT is relatively simple and easy. The problem comes in trying to get supervisors and other trainers to accept that people just don't remember things very well. We all are guilty of trying to remove the blame from ourselves for communication by stating forcefully, *"Don't you remember, I told you last week to do it this way!"* If we remember that we haven't done our training properly unless we can say, "Don't you remember, *you told me* last week it should be done this way," we'll do a lot better training. Perhaps this book will continue to help that happen . . .

M.M.B.

Decatur, Georgia
May 1994

PREFACE TO THE FIRST EDITION

When employees come on a new job, or when their job changes significantly, they must learn to do the job properly. Chances are that someone will do some training, if no more than saying, "The lathe is over there," or "The hours are eight to five." In most cases there will be a significant amount of training done in the beginning, with less and less being done as time goes by. The training may be done by the senior craftsman, the job leader, the first line foreman, or some supervisor assigned the task. So far as this book is concerned, it doesn't matter who does the training, because all of what is said has to do with what goes on between the "trainer" and "trainee." The *title* of the person doing the training and the *job* of the individual being trained are not as important as the *methods* used in preparing and carrying out the training.

The user of this book must realize that it will not solve all of his or her training problems. It will not do the work nor provide the follow-up and constant alertness that must come after the training has been done. The book will not keep the records that should be kept; it will not record the shortcomings of either the trainer or the trainee. In short, it is not a substitute for common sense and good judgment. However, the book will enable the person doing the training to take a better look at the task of trying to get someone else to do a job in an acceptable way. It will help the supervisor who wants a reasonably guaranteed method for improving an employee's performance.

Finally, it should be noted that there is no attempt to make a formal "textbook" rule or guide out of this. While much of the employee's training is done formally, the vast majority of what is learned comes from day-to-day contact with the person who is responsible for the work output (whether he be senior craftsman, foreman, or supervisor). The steps in on-the-job training are simple and easy to understand. They should not be thought of as things to follow only when a training program has been announced, or when large amounts of time have been set aside for training. The principles apply equally to changing a typewriter ribbon or to putting a new bit in a drill press. As a supervisor, you should learn the principles and practice them when the opportunity arises—even at home showing the children how to throw a football or teaching them to use the new kitchen stove. Then you should begin to use the principles on the job. Once you feel comfortable with them—and see the results—you will use the principles as a matter of habit. The success that follows will make all the learning and practice well worthwhile!

M.M.B.

Atlanta, Georgia
April 1969

ACKNOWLEDGMENT

The author wishes to acknowledge with thanks the courtesy of Resources for Education and Management, Inc., for permission to reproduce illustrations from an original set of filmstrips on on-the-job training.

PROLOGUE TO THE FOURTH EDITION

CHANGES OVER THE YEARS

On-the job training (OJT) still lacks a degree of "respectability" in training circles. It's sometimes associated with "dirt-under-the-fingernails" training, as opposed to the more exciting "management" training. It lacks the thrills of role playing, action mazes, games, or other "exotic" training methods. Yet, in all of this, there is the obvious strong need for teaching someone how to do a job that is usually done with the hands. Historically more studying has been done on how to do classroom training than on-the-job training. Over the years we have learned a considerable amount about how to do it, and the steps shown in this book attest to the fact that there are some right and wrong ways of doing it. It may be helpful to look at some changes in the last 50 years or so in our supervisory philosophies that affect the practice of on-the-job training.

In the early 1950s, under the guidance of Dr. George Odiorne, we embarked on a practice called "Management by Objectives" (MBO). This was the beginning of looking to people close to the job to tell us things about the job. The idea of MBO was—with oversimplification—to let the lowest levels of employees get involved in setting goals for the coming year about their own work and production, and determine how to measure this. Certain parameters were established by higher management, and then the various levels from the bottom up would determine how much and how well they would do in the coming year. It became pretty obvious that people worked harder at trying to meet goals they set for themselves than goals that were imposed upon them. This was the beginning of letting the workers get involved in decision making about their own jobs.

This assumed that everyone already knew their jobs and how to do them. It did not take into consideration that the employees might not know how to do their jobs as efficiently as possible. No provisions were made for letting the employees suggest better ways of doing the job, or at least having the supervisor being certain that the employees had the expertise and skills to do the job at its best. On the other hand, it assumed—properly so—that the employees knew how to do the job well enough, and that the design of the tasks were satisfactory. The end result was that not much training really took place. The workers did have good skills and thought the jobs were being done reasonably well. The fact was that they could have improved with further training, but the kind of training the supervisors were doing wasn't very efficient, though it was not thought to be bad at the time. The jobs themselves were quite simple, compared to today's technology, so training was not as much a consideration. Jobs or workers didn't change very much, either, so once a job was learned well by a worker, not much "updating" training was required.

When MBO was exported to Japan, it was beginning to be outdated in the United States but was received as a miracle in Japan. For the following years, it was used, improved, and finally exported back to us as "Quality Control Circles." It had various names, and more are being added each year, but basically it had the same philosophy of talking to the people closest to the job to find out things about the job. The difference was that it now became obvious that the workers can best tell us what is needed to improve the operation, efficiency, and production in the plant. (Gradually this has become "Total Quality Management" or some derivation of it.) Two things happened as a result of this new/old concept: First, it became obvious that the workers might be doing wrong things well, and right things poorly; second, if the workers were to improve the jobs, or make suggested changes in the job operation, they would have to be trained, often from ground zero.

OJT TAKES ON NEW RESPECTABILITY

Training was needed in a number of areas. First the seemingly unwieldy language and concepts of the Quality programs themselves required training. The employees needed to know how to fill out forms, return information, being sure to use the right nomenclature in every case (usually a near-foreign language to most). The supervisors—usually picked to lead the "circles" or team meetings—had little skill in conducting meetings, so they needed training. The hourly people involved in the meetings had no particular experience nor skill in working as team members, so they were not able to function well many times. But the real significance was that as the jobs changed or reorganization took place in the work operations, the employees needed a great deal of training in OJT. No one was particularly good at this kind of training, so the training often was done poorly—though not thought to be so by most.

This all goes back to the fact that we have studied so little about how to do OJT that it's even hard to identify what is good and what is bad training. The accepted consensus is that about 95 percent of the training supervisors do is so poor that the job suffers measurably, and both the supervisor and the trainee agree it is the trainee who is at fault, which is not correct. The bulk of the training is mostly show and tell, and then they are asked if there are questions—which there usually aren't—and then the trainee is told, "Okay, now you try it." Since it is so close to the training that retention is still good, the trainee does it fairly well, and the supervisor records that training has been done successfully. Since the trainee has done nothing to get it into his or her head—not doing any thinking and talking and repeating—little is done to embed the information into the brain.

As we'll see in this book, there are some specific skills required in order to do successful on-the-job training, which is unique and must be learned. It is not a matter of just knowing the job. It is not a matter of just telling and showing the employee what must be done. It is a matter of doing specific things in specific ways in order for the training to be successful.

ADDITIONAL CHANGES BRING MORE TRAINING NEEDS

With the advent of various government regulations, such as brought about with safety, health, environmental, and other considerations, training was pushed further into the forefront. In the past, just learning to do the job was complexity enough. Now, it's a matter of learning the job, but in terms of is it safe, environmentally correct, done with proper health considerations, etc.? Because we didn't always do the training, or put proper emphasis on it, the regulations now frequently specify what and how much training must be done. Interestingly enough, the consideration is very often on the curriculum rather than the methodology of the training. Lack of knowledge or specifications on what is good training has left it up to the individual trainers to determine the quality of the training. Training is often measured in terms of quantity instead of quality.

Organizations are beginning to take a notice of the *quality* of the training, since more is at stake than just production. Finally, people are realizing that there is good and bad training, made up not of how much the trainer knows but of how skilled he or she is at getting the message and skill across to the trainee. The good part of this is that the training is beginning to be based on what the trainee can do when the training is over, as opposed to what the trainer did during the training.

TRAIN-THE-TRAINEE APPROACH

Some organizations have found a way to ensure that the training is being done properly by training the trainees on how the training should be done. Essentially, they provide the trainees with the same kind of instruction they give the trainers, showing them the importance of getting the learner involved in saying and doing, instead of just looking and nodding. The advantage of this is that the trainees now know just what is expected of them and what they can expect from the trainer. In some cases, the trainee is allowed to judge just how well the training is done and can reject poor training by not agreeing to sign that the training has been done. With a very few exceptions, this had improved the training immensely, for obvious reasons. Knowing that the trainees have been trained, the supervisors or trainers are much more attentive to the OJT training as well as their own application of it when they are training.

chapter 1

WHY TRAIN?

It would be rather ridiculous to ask, "Is it really necessary to train people how to do their jobs?" No one would dare say no. It would be equally foolish to ask, "Is some training better than other training?" Here again, everyone would immediately answer in the affirmative. But suppose we were to ask the question: "How do you tell the difference between good and bad training?" Even though it is apparent that some of our training produces better results than other training, we aren't always able to tell exactly what makes the difference. Obviously, when we have an employee who is responsible for certain work, and we expect that work to be done properly, we want to have only the *good* kind of training, rather than the bad. *But we must find out what makes the difference.*

WHAT IS GOOD TRAINING?

It is much easier to define the *results* of good training than to define the *action* of good training. If, after training, the employee

can do what he couldn't do before the training, and if the training did not take too long nor cost too much, we conclude that the training was "good." On the other hand, if, when the training is over, the employee still cannot do the job for which she was trained, then the training may have been "bad." We say "may" because the training may have been all right, but other conditions, such as location, attitude of the employee, time of day, or the employee's lack of ability, may have made the training fail. While the person doing the training has a responsibility for these things, too, the actual instruction may have been good.

So we see that in trying to find out what good training and bad training are we must look, among many other things, at the results of the training and the conditions under which the training took place. Of course, it would be easy to say that good training is simply the kind of training that produces the results we want. But this wouldn't help us much if we were trying to learn how to train others. What we need to do, then, is to examine some *methods* and see how they work. Further, we need to use our own imagination and see whether there are better ways of doing what we are trying to do. After all, if we know the job well enough to train others, we ought to be very well suited to figuring out ways to improve the training method.

For the present we will say that good training is that training which produces the desired result, if the expense of time, energy, money, and so forth, isn't too great. This will give us a chance to discuss the things that influence the results and a chance to answer another question, "Why do we train at all?"

WHY DO WE TRAIN?

Poor Reasons for Training

Someone (who isn't very well informed) says, "We *always* train people on the job. It's just part of the job. We always have. . . . I guess we always will." Unfortunately this is true in many cases, but it isn't a very good reason for training. We don't always train in the right things; we don't always train at the right time; we don't always train the right people. But it does look as if we are always training somebody to do something.

Let's look at what happens if we train just because "we always have." This probably means we are still teaching the same subject, in the same way. But very few jobs that we do remain the same year in and year out. The job changes because equipment and methods change. The people change for better or worse for many reasons. Hiring policies change, so the company may be getting people who are more or less skilled than before, more or less capable than before, more or less intelligent than before. If our training hasn't changed, we probably aren't meeting the needs as well, even though at one time our training was doing a nearly perfect job. Since the job changes and the people change, just training because we always have isn't good enough.

Now we look at another reason for training: "The employees expect it." Why? Why do they expect to be trained regardless of the circumstances? They probably don't *all* expect this, but there must be a reason why some of them expect this kind of thing. They may think, like some supervisors, that "we always have had training, so I guess we always will have it." There is the possibility that they look forward to training because it is time off their regular jobs. No production is required. Someone else "catches" the line or fills in, so they are justifiably excused from doing their work. Neither of these is a very good reason for expecting training, and the results obtained from such training aren't likely to be very satisfactory. After all, *people who are "going along for the ride" can't be expected to settle down and learn new things for their job.*

There are other reasons given for training that aren't any more valid than the ones we have mentioned so far. "We train because the money is in the budget," or ". . . because time is allowed in the work schedule, and we have to report a certain amount of training on the monthly report." We admit, of course, that these reasons aren't always spoken in so many words, but actions speak much louder than words. This kind of attitude can be recognized by such things as scheduling training for the last "few" minutes of the day, or at other times when the employees aren't in the proper frame of mind. (For instance, right before lunch they worry more about whether they will get off in time for lunch than they do about learning whatever we are trying to teach.)

As we will see later in more detail, timing and attitude have much to do with the end result of the training effort and should be taken into account *every time* training is done. Sometimes there is even the situation where a certain amount of training has to be reported, and the person filling out the report feels inclined to exaggerate the actual time since not enough was done. Whether or not the person has really exaggerated isn't the point here. What does matter is that there ought to be a better reason for training, and certainly a stronger commitment by everyone—especially the one doing the training—as to the place and value of training. *It is as unfair to employees to falsify training records as it is to train them under such conditions that little or no learning can take place, and then to hold them accountable for results based on their knowledge of what was supposed to have been learned.*

Valid Reasons for Training

There are perhaps other reasons given for training that aren't good enough to justify the time, effort, and money, but let's look at some reasons why we *should* include training on the job. There are good reasons, and we should take them into consideration each time we consider the kind and amount of training to be done. One of the obvious reasons for training is that the *employees can't do something that the job requires should be done.* There is some skill they have yet to perfect or acquire, or some knowledge they are lacking that keeps them from doing a completely satisfactory job. If they are to be evaluated on using this skill or having this knowledge, and if they are thought to be capable of learning what is required, then this is reason enough

for training. Such a condition does more than merely justify the training. It makes training a *necessity*.

For example, if an employee has been working on a certain type of machine and is then moved to another machine that is similar, except that certain parts of the operation are slightly different, then we must assume the responsibility for seeing that the employee is trained to use this new machine properly. The fact that the employee could operate the last machine satisfactorily gives us reason to believe that he has the ability to handle this one if given the chance to learn about its operation. For this reason we should schedule the training, be sure that the conditions are right for the most learning to take place, and then do the necessary instructing.

The same things could be said, of course, if the employee stayed in the same place and the machine was changed. A newer or slightly different model is installed and the employee is expected to continue to produce satisfactorily. Again, we must assume that the employee can do the job with the different machine, but only if we see to it that proper training is provided. We must *avoid the tendency* of some "old-timers" who feel that the best way to learn is to *"throw them in over their heads—they'll learn to swim quickly enough!"* This may have been the way they learned, but it is by far the costliest and often the most inefficient

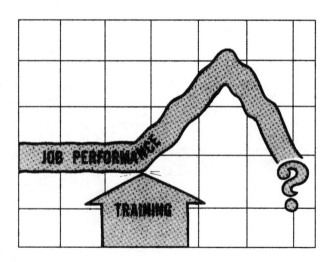

WHY DO WE TRAIN?   13

training method in the long run. *The scrap pile is full of waste from people "learning to swim" on the job without proper guidance.*

An equally good reason for training is that *an employee is doing something wrong.* Regardless of a worker's length of service, previous experience, or prior training, training should be considered if the job is being done incorrectly. As we will see later, the lack of training may not be the real problem. There may be an attitude problem or poor morale or personality conflicts or many other things. The reason for the incorrect job should be determined before a training program is started, but once it is decided that the *employee really can't do the job right because she doesn't know how,* then there should be training. Such training is not only justified but is a *necessity.*

Let's look at a particular situation. By some method—on-the-job inspection, looking at the rejection records, etc.—we find that a certain employee is not doing the work satisfactorily. After further investigation we decide that the reason is obvious: The employee is actually doing the job wrong. The employee is going through the motions, turning out the proper number of units, and perhaps is even happy with the production. *But the employee is doing the work wrong!* Before going to the employee and pointing out the errors (unless they are small and easily corrected), we would want to look at the employee's training record to see if he was ever trained on this particular operation before. We would also want to see if the job has changed since the employee was trained. If the job has changed, the reasons for the errors are obvious. But suppose the job is the same and the employee has been trained to do the job as it now is supposed to be done. How can we account for the errors creeping in? There are several points to consider in answering this question.

Maybe the errors haven't just "crept" in. Maybe they have been there for a long time. Maybe they were there under another supervisor who couldn't or wouldn't recognize them. Maybe the employee couldn't do the job right even after the training because the *training* wasn't good enough, hence not effective. (Note: We tend to state in training records that an employee has had training in such and such a course, but we fail to state the *caliber of teaching that was done.* In other words, all the accountability is placed on the employee, and none on the person doing the instructing.) All of this points out the need for good measurement techniques for our training programs, and frequent evaluations of the job performances of our people. It isn't enough just to know that an employee is doing the job wrong; *we need to know how long the employee has been doing it wrong, what steps have been taken to correct the errors, and what measurement was taken of the effectiveness of the training given to the employee.* Then we start our job training, *but not until then.*

We need to make a distinction here between the employee who is doing something wrong and the one who isn't doing it well enough or fast enough. In the first case the actual operation is being done wrong: The tube is bent crooked, the form has the figures in the wrong place, the nuts are tightened too tight, the customers are given the wrong information, and so forth. In the other case, the operation is all right, but something about the performance needs to be improved. The line is slowed because the employee takes too long to do the work, the numbers on the ledger aren't written clearly enough, the part is passed before it is polished to specifications, and so forth. In the case of doing the job wrong, it is easier to find out whether training is the problem than it is when the job isn't being performed up to standard. It is very hard to determine whether training will solve the problem in the latter case. But we will talk about this later. Right now we are looking for reasons for training and whether the employee is doing the job well enough. If we have decided that training will help, then this is a perfectly justifiable reason for spending the time and effort to train. Again, it is not only justified but necessary!

Retraining

Another very good reason for training is that a job is being phased out but it is desirable to keep the employee. In this case, retraining is necessary. Ideally, some job could be found that will use skills similar to those required for the job. Then the training task will be much simpler. Regardless of the new job to be learned, however, the training method discussed in Chapter 8 will be used. Right now let's mention the attitude of the supervisor or person doing the instructing. If there ever is a case where the instructor should *not* take the training job lightly, it is in retraining. In many ways, the situation is like hiring a new person. *We recognize the need for training a new employee. We ought to see the need for retraining an old employee just as quickly.* It isn't enough to say, "We'll put Charlie on the form press. He's a sharp fellow and should be able to pick that up pretty quickly." Then after we have put him there, we say to Charlie, "If you have any problems, let me know." We have created the problem by moving Charlie; we should take the necessary steps to solve it without waiting for Charlie to make mistakes and even get a reputation as an unsatisfactory employee. Put simply, this means that we have another perfectly good reason for training.

Deficiency

When it comes right down to it, all of this could be condensed to the simple fact that *we train because there is a deficiency, or an expected deficiency.* If we think in terms of deficiencies, we are more likely to come up with good training. And we're more likely to train for the right reasons. If we look at our employees and ask the simple question, *"What is it they can't do?"* the picture gets a lot clearer. We don't go off on the tangent of training because we always have, or because the employees expect it, or the money is in the budget, or any of the reasons we've discussed so far. It'll help us, too, when we think about the job analysis we have to do and setting standards for the job we're training on. It all comes together in simple formula: *Job Requirement – Employee Skill = Deficiency.* Let's look at this formula for a little while.

Many times we say that a person needs training because the job isn't getting done. As simple as that sounds, *that may not be a deficiency.* What do we mean by "not getting the job done"? Do we mean that the job isn't getting done as well as the last employee on the job did it? Or as well as *we* did it when we were on the job? Or as well as someone up the line would like to have it done, without really knowing what's involved in getting the job done? As we'll see later, *setting job standards is an important part of the supervisor's job, and one that must come before training.* There is an old Hindu saying to the effect that "If you don't know where you're going, any road will get you there." Before we get too far down the road of training, we have to ask ourselves, "Do I know where I'm going?" If we don't know what a good job is, then we won't know if we've been successful or not. Neither will we know whether or not the employee is successful as a trainee.

But, let's face it, when we walk by an employee who's not doing the job, what do we do? Most of us stop, correct the employee, show the proper way it should be done, and go our way thinking we've done some training . . . and maybe we have. But maybe we haven't! Unless we've been practicing proper ways of training, we may have done a bad job of training, and yet tomorrow when we walk by again and see the error still being practiced, we may decide the employee just hasn't got it. We've done an injustice to the employee but aren't likely to blame the poor performance on ourselves. But to make it worse, we may even have known where the employee was in the operation. Was there a standard? Does the employee know that standard now? Did we bother to explain it in that way to the employee? If we didn't, then we have no right to expect the employee to perform correctly tomorrow. What we see happening in this example is a case where we start at the wrong end of the formula: We start with the *deficiency*, rather than the *job standard*, or job requirements. *All training should start with the job requirements*, as we'll see later. Looking at our formula, we go now to the *employee's skill*. We still haven't gotten to the deficiency yet!

It's no easy task to find out just what the employee knows and can do. Most organizations have some kind of appraisal plan. These plans tell how well the employee is performing and perhaps what the employee's future with the organization holds. These are made up once a year and often just filed away. The employee may or may not know what the appraisal says. The employee may or may not have a chance to go over the material with the supervisor. The employee may or may not get a chance to express his or her views ahead of the appraisal time as to how the job is going. We won't even try to go into appraisal systems—their worth or lack of it. But we do want to make it clear that a *good appraisal*—one that goes into great detail once a year—*probably isn't enough to base training on*. We have to *know a lot about the person's capability, performance,* and *weaknesses on each specific phase of the job* before we can determine the person's real performance level. And we can't wait until appraisal time to do the training. Notice we keep talking about the employee's skill, not just the *lack* of skill. We really need to know what the employee *can do*, as well as what the employee *can't do*. (By the way, as we'll talk about in more detail later, it's a good idea to *let our employees know that they have some skills and that we recognize that fact*. We can easily discourage them if we point out only things they are doing wrong.)

As we look again at the formula, we see that once we've found out what the job is, and what the employee is able to do, we can go to the *deficiency*. The difference between what we want and what the employee can give is the deficiency that we must overcome in order for the employee to do the job satisfactorily. Many times we tend to say that the deficiency and the training requirements are the same. This isn't necessarily so. It may be that training isn't the answer, at least not to all deficiencies. It may be that some deficiencies will be worked out on the job with just a little guidance. It may be that we can suggest areas of improvement to the employee and let the employee do the rest. There's always the possibility that the employee doesn't even know what we expect and doesn't know that we think there is a deficiency. It is also a possibility that this will be all that will be needed. When the employee finds out that something is wrong, the behavior may change immediately. *There are many cases where the employees could have been doing the job the right way as easily as the wrong way, but nobody ever told them that they weren't doing the job correctly.*

There's another situation where we wouldn't train, even when there is a deficiency. *If the deficiency is such that it takes practice to improve or to meet the standard, then we let time take care of the overcoming, rather than training.* This is particularly true of manual skills, since practice—more than anything else—makes the difference. Training sets the standard for *procedure*; practice sets the standard for *production*. However, even in jobs that require customer contact, training won't always take the place of practice. Training is needed, to be sure, but it won't lead to perfection. Only practice will do that. For example, it's easy enough for us to tell an employee that the customer is always right, but it takes a lot of practice in dealing with an unhappy customer before it becomes natural to *smile* instead of *frown* when we hear harsh words from an angry customer. Here, again, *we have to know what we want of the employee. It won't happen automatically.* There will be behavior of some kind, but if the employee isn't told what is the right behavior under these conditions, it probably won't be the kind we want.

So we have to decide whether or not the deficiency can be made upon the job. Even if part of it can be overcome without training—and that seems to be the efficient way to do it—we should do it that way by all means. There is enough training that has to be done without doing that which isn't necessary. *The good supervisor will make the training count each time*, always looking for ways of overcoming the deficiency without spending more time than required.

THE PLACE OF TRAINING

Earlier we asked the question, "Why do we train?" We have seen a number of good reasons from the employee's standpoint. There are also reasons for training from the supervisor's standpoint, and from the company's point of view as well.

First of all, if first-line supervisors have it listed or implied as part of their job that they are responsible for the training of their employees, then training is not something they can ignore, any more than they can fail to turn in reports, neglect to keep track of production, or stop assigning work. In other words, training is just as much a part of their job as these other activities, and if they fail to do the training, then they are doing just as poor a job as if they had failed to do the other things usually associated with their work. The supervising clerk would not think of assigning work to all but one of the people in the typing pool, letting that one sit idle. But neither should the supervisor let one of the employees go along without the necessary training. If supervisors fail in either of these things, they are not doing what their job requires and are themselves *unsatisfactory employees.* One problem that supervisors have is that they are sometimes unable to put training in its proper place. They fail to think of it as a *regular* part of their job, and so put it off "until I can take time from my *real* job." However, *training is a real and important part of the supervisor's work.*

From a "value to the company" standpoint it is also a very important matter. When employees know how to do their jobs, they can do them better. When they can do their jobs better, they can produce more (perhaps faster and better), and hence the company can make more money. This same money, in the long run, comes back to benefit both the supervisor and the employee who has been trained.

The Need for Greater Technological Training

Much technical training is being provided by schools such as vocational/technical schools. However, it is important that organizations train people technically to do the specific job being asked of them—even for the simplest tasks, such as electrical work, or wiring of some kind, or assembling equipment, even where skill has been obtained before coming to the job. Each organization does it differently. It is therefore important that the organization train that employee in the way that the organization wants the job done. Put another way, even the most technical job is done slightly differently in each organization. Jobs are becoming more and more technical, complex, and specific. It is not fair to the organization nor to the employee to expect the new hire to come off the street, even with a certificate in hand as being a qualified worker, and conform to the organization's standards immediately. Each organization has certain standards, certain traditions, even some idiosyncrasies that are unique enough that there must be training to satisfy the job requirements. A very simple example would be the position of file clerk. While there are courses to teach filing and there are identified filing systems, each organization files to its own standard. Each boss frequently files to his or her standards. You get the work done much quicker and much better with more satisfaction for the employee if the new employee is given training to meet these unique requirements.

TRAINING AND THE NEW EMPLOYEE

In many ways, *new employees are at the mercy of the supervisor and the organization*. If they choose to do training, then the employees have a chance to learn the job and be successful. *If they choose not to train, the employees are left to their own devices and generally make poor employees the rest of their careers.* They have little recourse against the supervisor or the organization, and to make it worse, *these new employees will likely get blamed for doing a poor job.* Obviously they deserve training. *In all fairness to them, they shouldn't be held accountable for jobs for which there has been no training.* But even if this wasn't so, the supervisor and the organization should want as much good training done as possible: the supervisor because she will get inferior job performance, costing time and effort to redo or correct the mistakes made; the organization because poor performance is costly in lost service, production, and/or time. What happens if the training doesn't get done? Let's notice some of the prospects.

The Job Is Learned Incorrectly

Employees will make some effort to do something on the job. *They will try to figure out the procedures on their own, which is usually incorrect.* They will think about previous jobs or use logic or just start moving switches or twisting dials or pushing buttons until something happens. *By the time some training comes along, they will have learned many bad habits that will stay with them for a long time.* Throwing people in over their heads is a way of teaching people to swim, but it is also a way of drowning people.

Learning from Watching Others

Studies show that the majority of employees end up learning their jobs by asking other employees how to do the work. From operating cash registers to working on an assembly line to serving customers, *the most often used method of training is watching someone else do the job,* and *maybe asking questions.* There is some irony when an employee is left to learn by watching others, with no help from the supervisor, then have the supervisor come along and ask, "Who ever told you to do it *that* way?" If the new employees learn from the older, experienced employees, but there is no accountability or prestige to be had in doing the training, it will be a bad situation. *Certainly the employees will learn some things, many of them correctly, but they will also learn some errors or shortcuts that aren't approved or correct.* There is also a good chance that some unsafe things will be taught that will take a career to unlearn!

Insufficient Training

Perhaps the worst offense occurs when the supervisor gives an overview with a promise of more extensive training later, but the "later" never comes. *The employees learn a little, and now they're left with "training" on their records. If they fail, the boss will point to the initial training effort as a way of saying that training was actually done, without regard to the quality or quantity.*

Finally, let's notice that poor training or no training at all is unfair to the employee, because a future is at stake. Most people who study motivation have concluded that *poorly trained employees quickly lose interest and become unmotivated.* This is translated into disinterest and goes on the record as a bad appraisal. While it is true that the employees probably *are* unmotivated, nevertheless the cause of *the lack of motivation lies with the supervisor, not the employees.* Of course, it is generally accepted that the employee, not the supervisor, will be blamed for the poor motivation! It is also unfair to the organization not to train new employees. It costs a lot of money to recruit, screen, interview, hire, and place employees on the payroll. With this investment, the organization deserves to get the most out of this new resource as possible. Not training is poor use of raw material, and there is never an excuse for such behavior!

TRAINING THE EXPERIENCED SUPERVISOR

Jobs Change

Even though it is often quoted, it is still true that the only thing in any job that is constant is change. Jobs change. Standards change. Procedures change. Technologies change. As we've seen in this chapter, the only way the successful organization can survive is to train its employees to meet these changes. While we recognize the need to train new employees, we should be equally ready to train experienced employees as well. We're not just talking about traditional retraining, that is, training an employee who has forgotten how to do a job, nor are we talking about the employee who has never done the job correctly. We're saying that jobs gradually change as new pieces of equipment are added, as shortcuts are developed, and as small modifications are made in the product being produced. Often the training is no more than a few words from the supervisor to say, "We no longer do this in that manner, but we now do it this way." While it might constitute training, if this is done often over a period of time, the employee will gradually become less and less competent. For that reason, we need to train the employee on the new changes.

Employees Change

While it is obvious that the jobs are changing all the time, we overlook the fact that employees, in fact, are also changing. They change in two ways. First, they gain greater skills. They gain a greater understanding of the job itself. They understand why the job is being done the way it's being done. They understand the end product. When they first came to work they only did what they were trained to do and didn't really know what the end product was. This means that the employee has a better knowledge of the job and has changed enough to handle some more training, perhaps to perform better in the present job or to grow into another job. Second, employees change because they have developed bad habits, shortcuts, easy ways, and even unsafe ways of doing the job. If the supervisors have allowed this to happen, they've created a situation where the employee is doing something without even being aware of it—that's not the satisfactory way to perform. Even if the end product looks the same, the work itself may be done unsafely or in a haphazard way that could produce error, waste, and/or accidents. This is another reason why we need to train experienced employees.

CONCLUSION

Why do we train? Not because we "always have" or "the employees expect it." There needs to be a better reason for training and a stronger commitment by everyone to the value of training. One of the obvious reasons for training is that the employees are not able to do something that the job requires of them. Another good reason is that an employee is doing something incorrectly. Training is also necessary if jobs are being phased out but it is desirable to keep the employees for new jobs, for which training is needed.

When it comes right down to it, we train because there is a deficiency or an expected deficiency (because of change in personnel or procedures). If we think in terms of deficiency, we are more likely to train for the right reasons, and we're also more likely to come up with good training.

QUESTIONS FOR SMALL GROUP DISCUSSIONS

1. What is good training?

2. How can we tell the difference between *good* training and *bad* training?

3. Whose responsibility is it to see that employees get proper training?

4. Do all employees deserve training? Discuss.

5. Why do we train employees?

6. Who benefits from training?

7. What are some reasons given for training that really don't justify the time and energy spent on training?

8. Pick a training course that you regularly conduct (on the job or off) and list the *real* reasons you teach it. How many of these reasons are justifiable?

9. Why should first-line supervisors be held accountable for seeing that their people get trained?

10. What are the advantages of on-the-job training over "throwing them in over their heads and letting them learn to swim"?

chapter 2

WHY AND HOW PEOPLE LEARN

WHY PEOPLE LEARN

It is interesting to try to make a list of reasons why people learn. It might not seem important to supervisors to know *why* people learn, since all they care is that people *do* learn, regardless of the reasons why. But it does make a difference. Since people learn for different reasons, our approach to getting them to learn may have to be different with each of the people we are trying to instruct. Fortunately, we don't have to be professional psychologists to understand why people learn. Ask almost any group of people *why people learn* and you will get a list that looks something like this:

- They want to.
- Their boss makes them.
- They are curious.
- They want to know more than someone else.
- They are afraid of losing their job.
- They want self-satisfaction.

- They want to make more money.
- They can't help it.
- They want to prove to others that they can learn.
- They are ashamed not to.

The list could go on, but the answers would begin to look alike. Some of the items aren't very specific, but some of them are perfectly clear. We might try to break them down into categories:

- Fear
- Curiosity
- Self-satisfaction
- Social pressures
- Economic values
- Reward

Let's look at some examples. *Some people seem to have an inborn curiosity that never gets satisfied.* They are always learning new things, whether on the job or off. They learn about dogs or seashells or the stars or gems or anything that they don't already know about. On the other hand, there are those that learn just enough about their job to get by, but no more. They show no interest in the world about them. (Incidentally, they are not necessarily "dull" people, nor ignorant; they just don't have a great

deal of curiosity.) There are those who strive to learn a little bit about a lot of things, if for no other reason than to be able to *impress others*. They rarely ever study anything in much depth. Some people are motivated to learn because the more they learn, the more money and status they stand to get. In other words, *their interest in learning is purely economic.* Into this same category fall those who learn because they can't afford to lose their job, and they worry a great deal about any change in the job. Any change represents a threat to their security because they are afraid someone else will get the job, or the job will be done away with, or they won't be able to learn the new routine.

Thinking back on the examples we have discussed, we might narrow the reasons why people learn to just three basic classes:

- Desire for reward
- Fear of punishment
- Curiosity

Any example or reason we think of will fit into one of these three categories. (Go back over the examples given and see which of the three categories each one fits into.)

Now let's see what all of this has to do with on-the-job training. We need to ask ourselves, "Since people learn for different reasons, should they be instructed differently?" The answer to this may sound a bit strange. In reality, we train the same but we *approach* the training differently and we view the *results* differently. *During the training, things may come up that we can better understand if we know why a person learns.* For instance, the employee may ask, "Do I *have* to know that?" The answer may be "No," and we may be disgusted because the employee ought to be interested in the bit of information we were trying to present. Someday the employee may need the information. But if we realize that this particular employee is learning just enough to get by, and in the process really does learn enough to do the job *satisfactorily*, then we will avoid getting frustrated or disgusted. After all, we are not paying employees to do something "someday," nor are we training them for an eventual job. *We may also want to look at our own training goals and see if we are putting too much emphasis on "interesting things" and not enough on things that are required on the job.*

We can use the information in this chapter on why people learn without going too deeply into their motives and without passing judgment upon them. Very simply, people indeed have reasons for what they do, and basically they are trying to satisfy some kind of "need" when they do it. This is true for other things besides learning. We buy something because we are convinced it will fill a need. Any good salesperson knows this. Picture the inexperienced salesperson who comes in and unveils a "handy dandy little widget maker." She puts it on the table, plugs it in, turns it on, pushes several buttons, turns the crank, and out comes a handful of widgets! The demonstration has been flawless. The machine worked just as she said it would, and you are convinced it will make perfect widgets every time. But you don't buy the machine. Why? Because the salesperson failed to show you how this little widget maker fills any *need* you have. The best you can do is to tell her, "If I ever find anyone who knows what a widget is and needs one, I'll surely tell her where to buy a widget maker!"

The thing that the salesperson omitted in her approach was showing that you had a need, then showing that her product would fill this need better than anything else at the price offered. "Would you like to cut costs, save time, win friends, look smart, talk better?" All of these things appeal to *needs*. Then when the product is introduced, it is a simple matter to show that it matches up with the need. Once it can be shown that the product solves the problem (meets the need), the rest is downhill. *So it is with training. We must find a way to show that the training will fill a need that we have pointed out.* Many times we do our training like the inexperienced salesperson, by introducing the product (the new method or correct way) before we have established that there is a need. In essence, *we must answer the employee's question, "What's in it for me*?" When we talk later (in Chapter 7) about preparing for training, we will look at some ways to do this.

WHY PEOPLE DON'T WANT TO LEARN

This brings us to another important point: Why is it that sometimes people do not learn? We have seen reasons why people want to learn; now let's look at the other side.

Lack of Motivation

One obvious answer is that they just aren't motivated. They lack interest or enthusiasm. If this is the case, then we may be back to the same things we discussed under reasons for learning—we must find something to motivate them. But good motivation alone isn't a completely satisfactory solution. There are reasons why employees don't have an interest in learning, even after the advantages of learning have been pointed out to them. Sometimes the fault lies with the person doing the instructing rather than with the employee being trained. If supervisors put the training off until the very last part of the day because they aren't interested in it; if they have made it clear to *their* bosses that they don't really think that training is part of their job; if they enter into the training session with an attitude of "Let's get this over with and get on to something important"; if these statements represent the supervisors' attitude, then it isn't likely that their employees will be jumping with joy about receiving training.

On the other hand, if the person doing the training comes on strong with enthusiasm, such an attitude is probably going to influence the people being trained. If supervisors make it clear that training is part of their job and they want to do just as well

at that as at any other part of their job; if they allow proper time for training, and put it on an even plane with production, reporting, etc.; if they go about training in a skillful way; if they make sure that training is done at a time in the workday when it will be the most effective; if they make it clear to *their* bosses that they expect to be allowed to do the training correctly, even if it means fighting for a little more time and money; if supervisors do all these things, then they can't help but increase the interest and enthusiasm of the employees being trained. In fact, these things are *basic requirements for successful training*!

Another way supervisors can cause the people being trained to lose their interest and motivation is to do a *poor job of training*. All of us have experienced times when we were interested in learning something either on the job or in a classroom, only to find that the instructor did such a poor job that our interest turned to boredom or disgust. We finally became interested in only one thing: getting out of the training course. (Of course, a prime purpose of this book is to help people do a better job of training their employees!) *Poor training not only doesn't help employees do their jobs better, but it also makes them dislike the idea of receiving any training in the future.*

There is not much excuse for consistently poor instruction. There are specific skills that can be learned, practiced, and perfected. Being a good instructor is not something you either have or haven't got. It is somewhat like operating a lathe or a computer or a card punch. Some people have more aptitude for it than others, but most of us can learn the skill if we try. An instructor *who has both skill and enthusiasm makes it a lot easier for the employee to learn.*

Lack of Background

Another reason why employees don't learn as fast as we would like is that they don't have the necessary background to pick up the training. *What we may consider a lack of talent may be only a lack of experience.* Before we write employees off as incapable of doing their jobs, we should make sure that they have the background to absorb the instruction. How many times have we watched a guided tour through a plant and heard the person in charge say something like, "The residue comes from the acid bath into the oxidation tanks where the discharger controls the injection to prevent a flame-out temperature condition from developing. An improper balance between the anthracene and air will cause the destructive distillation process to produce impurities. *Now, are there any questions?*" The people in the group, completely unfamiliar with any of the terms being used, stand on one foot, then the other, waiting to move on. Probably the guide understood the process and may have thought the group did too. Even so, the guide did not produce any great amount of interest and certainly not very much learning! The group simply lacked the background to absorb what was said. The truth of the matter is they may not even know enough to ask questions, and to make it worse they may not know that they don't know.

A little reflection may show us that we have done the same thing with our employees. This most often happens when they are new, because there are so many things they don't know, but it also happens when they have been around for a long time. We may be like the tour guide: We understand what we are saying and *think* our employees do too, but our employees are not really learning. *We have to start where they actually are, not where we think they ought to be or where we assume they are.* The methods of training we talk about later on (in Chapter 8) will help us not to fall into this trap. What we have to look for is constant *feedback to see that the employees are following what we are saying.* When the feedback shows that they aren't with us, we change our course of action and try something else. Without the feedback from the employees, we have no chance of knowing how effective we are with our training. The *burden is on the person doing the training to see that it is done at the proper level.* It should not be left up to the employees to say that the training is over their head. This is sort of like saying to them, "This is where you should be, but if you are stupid, let me know, and I'll try something else."

Rebellion

We have to admit that some people do not learn because of a certain amount of *rebellion against authority that exists in all of us.* In severe cases it comes out as, "You represent the management, so train me if you think you can. But you won't get any help from me." Most of the time it isn't that bad, but we need to realize that the problem can and does exist. Now we get back to the idea of doing a little selling. *Show the employees what's in it for them.* This, combined with enthusiasm and interest on the part of the supervisor doing the training, will usually overcome any rebellious attitude. We just have to admit to ourselves that not all employees are sitting around hungrily waiting for us to train them. If they resent the company, they resent being trained. If they are not motivated to do the job, they will not be too motivated by the training. If they feel the company is getting all the benefits from their training and they aren't getting anything from it, they will rebel at the idea of learning more about the job. Supervisors can overcome much of this by the things we have already talked about (for example, by their own enthusiasm and skill, by telling the employees what they stand to gain from the training, by pitching the training at the employees' own level) and by using some of the ideas that will be presented later in this book.

Along with the idea of rebellion against authority, there is the *fear of having to learn something new.* The thought of moving to something unfamiliar may also cause employees to rebel. The excuses they use may not reveal the real reason behind their reluctance to receive the training. "I don't think the company has a right to require me to learn this" may really mean, "I don't know if I can learn this new job. I know how to do what I'm doing now, but I may not be able to handle the new job." If supervisors don't realize that this rebellion is really just a cover-up for a fear of change, they may spend a lot of time trying to convince their employees that the company *does* have the right to train them on something new. The time could be better spent in assuring them that they will be able to handle the job and that the training program will make it possible for them to do the work without any trouble.

Failure to Relate Training to the Job

Any time there is any training, whether it is done in the classroom or on the job, *every effort should be made to relate the training to the job as closely as possible.* One reason employees *don't learn is that they fail to see the relationship between what they are supposed to learn and what they will be doing when the training is over.* They rarely are satisfied with a statement like, "You may not see where this fits in, but take my word for it." Neither will they accept, "Go ahead and learn this because someday you may have to use it on the job." In other words, the employees respond best to the *"here and now."* They respond the least to what appears to have very little or nothing to do with their job as they see it right now.

But the training should relate directly to the job not only in content; it should *look the same way the job looks, feel the same way the regular job feels, smell the same, sound the same, etc.* If employees are to use their right hand when operating a machine on the line, then they should operate it with their right hand during the training. If a model or mock-up is made, it should look and respond just like the real thing it represents. If the employees will get grease on their hands on the job, they should get grease on their hands during the training. If the employees will be reaching for letterheads with their left hand when doing production work, the paper should be on their left side while they are learning to do the job. If the employees determine the proper setting of the machine from a worn black book, then they should use that same worn black book when they are training. *The*

employees shouldn't have to change anything when they start to do the real thing. If the training is intended to show them how to do the job, then everything about the training should be as close to the real job as possible. If it is, then they won't have to "unlearn" and then learn something else when they start to produce. The principle may be simple, but it is one of the most important rules to remember when setting up the training. *Always make the training situation as much like the real job as possible. It may mean the difference between a successful training job and a failure.*

WHY DON'T PEOPLE LEARN?

Sometimes we find ourselves in what should be a great learning situation. There is an obvious need for the employees to learn the skill. We've explained the goals of the training, even made some good objectives that predict the outcome of the learning experience. We've found the right place for the training and have made certain there will be no interruptions. We have the equipment ready and working. Then we find that the employees aren't mentally ready or don't seem interested or enthusiastic. Indeed, during the training effort we find some resistance, or at least some lethargy, and we wonder why they aren't as excited about the learning experience as we are. There are some reasons, and it is important for us to consider them in order to overcome the problems.

Like so many other things, success at learning breeds more success. If we've been successful at learning in the past, found it stimulating and rewarding to learn something we weren't familiar with, or have overcome some obstacles to learn it, then we are ready for the next challenge. The same is true of being *unsuccessful* at learning. When we are used to having unrewarding experiences at learning, we rarely look forward to another learning experience. *It is not surprising that we sometimes get employees who have never had success at learning.* For whatever reason, they just never have been good learners. They found school boring or teachers uninteresting. They didn't enjoy the homework or the class periods. Teachers may have been hard on them, or parents may not have been supportive of their learning efforts. Whatever the cause, learning just wasn't very exciting in their lives.

Now they find themselves in a learning situation that is not of their own choosing. There is nothing personal about it. It isn't us that they resent. It probably isn't the job they're unhappy with. *They just don't like being in a learning situation, and when they are, they revert back to their earlier days of disinterest, or disdain.*

Can we overcome this problem? Actually, there are things we can do that will work well and probably create more enthusiasm than we expect. Fortunately, we don't have to be psychologists or psychoanalysts in order to solve the problem. What we do with the kind of situations we've been describing is something we should consider for any questionable learning environment. We need to see that there are ample opportunities to allow the employees to demonstrate their learning capabilities. Put simply, *they need some successes at learning.* On the job there are so many chances for us to provide opportunities for success. Since the people we've hired have already demonstrated their competency in some ways, we have only to let them learn some more things and then let them know they've learned. *The key: Let them know they've learned.* Whenever they learn even the smallest things, there is the opportunity to give them a positive experience, such as a simple, "That's great. Now that you've learned that, let's go on to the next thing." We can include this encouragement in the preparation, too. We should talk about the future learning in terms of their past learning. "Since you've learned these things so well in the past, we've decided to go on with the next phase." It usually isn't enough to say something like, "I know you won't have any problem learning this," because they may feel they know more about their ability to fail than we do. *It's always better to show their success in learning than just to predict success for the future.*

There are other reasons why people aren't ready to learn, of course, and again, the problem isn't impossible to solve. Some have had bad learning experiences *on the job.* They have had supervisors who weren't very good trainers, but who still expected perfect performance after the training was over. These kinds of bad experiences leave their mark on employees, and rightly so. The most obvious solution is to offer better training. Just as when we are trying to let the employee have some successes by getting quick successes in small bites, we can also give them good training in quick, small bites. Let them see that they are learning, that the learning is good, and that the skill learned is usable. It won't take long for this to prove to the trainees that they can expect good training from now on and overcome the bad impressions given by previous training efforts.

Another thing that often causes employees to become discouraged or disenchanted with training is *training done in inappropriate environments*. It is often hard to find a place free of noise and distraction that has the reality of the job. The best kind of on-the-job training is done with real equipment or in a place that looks as much like the real place as possible. As discussed in other chapters, some employers provide places for training where there is equipment—or adequate simulations of the equipment—and space and quiet similar enough to the actual workplace to give the feel of the true environment. When this hasn't been the case, the employees may have been trained in areas where there are other employees standing around watching, where there is so much noise the supervisor's instructions couldn't be heard, or where the distractions have kept good learning from taking place. Here, again, the solution is obvious: Find a place that's not like this and let the employee experience something better.

HOW DO PEOPLE LEARN?

The questions of how people learn is too complex to consider thoroughly at this point, but there are some things we can note now that will help us to instruct others. The single most important thing to remember is that *the kind of learning we want in on-the-job training is never passive in nature*. That is, it is *learned by the employee doing something, not being told* to do something. It is called *active learning*. They key word is involvement. We might tell employees, "Tighten the nut until it slips when lightly held between your thumb and forefinger," but if they don't tighten some nuts until they get the exact feeling, they aren't likely to really learn what we are talking about. If we tell the clerk, "File the blue sheets by dates, the pink sheets alphabetically by signatures, the white sheets in reverse order by code number and place, and any unsigned sheets in the reject box," but don't get him involved in doing the practice and explaining the process back to us, we can't have any assurance that the procedure has been learned very well. The chances are very good, in fact, that the clerk will not remember what we said long enough to try it even once after we have left!

Simple Learning Process

It would be incorrect to say that there is only one kind of learning or that a person learns in only one way. *The truth is, people differ, and different people learn in different ways.* There are certain things that cause people to learn better, and that's what we really want to learn about. It's possible for someone to learn by making terrible mistakes. They won't forget the experience. But is that the best way to learn? There are those who say that the best way to learn to swim is to be tossed in the water and let nature take its course. The trouble with this argument is that we have a hard time explaining why so many people drown each year "because they couldn't swim"! In the adult world, we know better than to risk life and limb on such a silly process. We can't afford to risk the equipment or the machinery. We can't afford to lose our customers while the new employee discovers that certain responses don't please the customers very well. And there is another reason why the "trial and error" method shouldn't be used very often: There is always the danger that the employee will learn to do something wrong and *have trouble unlearning that behavior.* We tend to remember our first impressions, and if the first thing we remember is the wrong thing, then we've got a problem.

When we get to the chapter on how to do on-the-job training, we'll see a specific approach that has been tested for years and works better than any other method we know of right now. It takes into account the need for getting the learner involved, and also the idea of letting the employee see and do only the correct method of operation. *A third important aspect of this method is that it allows the employee to get the process in her head before getting it into her hands.* The reason we remember something is that we have somehow been able to register it in the brain. We learn some things without getting them into the mind, of course, but these things are dangerous in the business world, because they are sort of unchecked as they are put in. For example, if we want an operation to be done a certain way *for a certain reason*, we had better be sure that the employee doesn't just learn it mechanically. If something goes wrong and a change is required in the action, the employee will be in trouble. *Most supervisors want thinking employees, but they don't always train in a way that gives them that.* Many times the supervisor just tells the employee what needs to be done, then perhaps demonstrates, and then says, "Okay, you do it." As you will see in Chapter 8, this isn't the way to start the employee thinking!

What do we know for sure about learning? We've already talked about involvement. What else do we know? *We know that a person is more likely to remember things that came at a time when the information or skill was seen as needed*, rather than at a time when *the instructor said there is a need*. It has been said that *learning is a self-activity that starts with a problem and ends with a solution*. As philosophical as that sounds, it pretty well makes the point we want to make here. Why should a person learn anything? Why should a person decide to remember something—that is, decide to expend the effort required to learn it? We have talked about reasons why we teach and why people learn, but what we're talking about here is, when it comes right down to it, what makes one person decide to put out some effort to listen, to study, perhaps to ask some questions, when another person, even someone on the same kind of job, doesn't care to do these things? The reasons may vary, but they all end up being close to the fact that *we learn when we see that it fills some need*. And that's important not only from a motivational standpoint, but from a learning standpoint. If we want to be more sure that a person is going to retain the information, we must make sure that a need is present: That's a learning principle.

What else do we know? Well, we know that even when there is a need, *trainees will remember better what they said during the training than what was said by the trainer*. As trainers, we tend to want to do all the talking to make sure the employee gets the information just right. But what we're suggesting here is that the *trainees will do better to hear the words come out of their own mouths than out of ours*. This gives us two immediate advantages: The involvement fixes the information in the memory of the employees, and when we hear the things said, we get some *feedback* on how well the message got through. This feedback helps us gauge our own effectiveness in communicating.

As we will see later, *we have to overcome the temptation to do all the talking, all the action, all the thinking*. There is a measure of how well we have done in the training: Tomorrow, when we pass by the employee, can we say, *"Don't you remember, yesterday you told me . . ."* or do we have to say, *"Don't you remember, yesterday I told you . . ."*? If all we can say is that we've done all the telling, we haven't done a very good job of training. If we can say that the employee has told us something, then we've gotten some involvement and can feel more satisfied with our efforts.

In Chapter 8 we will talk in more detail about how to get this involvement. There are some specific steps we can learn. For now, let's just be sure to understand that the old idea of "learning by doing" is still good, but it must not be done in a careless, unplanned way. That's the trouble with just letting employees learn by themselves, without any guidance; they practice *error* more than *correctness*. Practically nothing we learn to do is a direct result of only hearing. Just about everything is the result of *seeing or doing*.

Avoid Future Grief from Bad Habits

Employees learn bad habits. They bring bad habits to the job. They learn them from other employees and they develop their own. Training is a way of preventing this from happening. If we don't train new employees or we allow older employees to continue to develop bad habits, we're creating some grief for ourselves, because the time is going to come when those bad habits will haunt us. While it is obvious that, if we allow people to continue to develop bad habits before they learn the correct way of doing the job, they may do the job in an unsafe manner. It is equally important that we keep people from developing these bad habits because bad habits are hard to break. It takes much longer to defeat bad habits than it does to teach the correct process in the beginning. It has been rightly said that practice makes permanent, not perfect. The longer a person uses a bad habit, does a job improperly, takes shortcuts, or whatever, the harder it will be to get that person out of those habits. The bad part about it is that all evidence suggests that even after they've been trained, employees in a crisis may revert back to the bad habits they had without thinking.

CONCLUSION

What makes a person learn? *Curiosity, fear, hope of reward?* Skillful instructors know that one or more of these is basic to the employees' desire to learn. They point out to the employees how the training will benefit them (not just how it will benefit the company). They exhibit enthusiasm for the training program, and the employees catch their enthusiasm. They use good teaching skills, and they start teaching at the employees' own level. Sometimes employees are rebellious, and the instructor has to "sell" them the training program; but often a rebellious attitude is just a cover-up for the fact that the employees are afraid to learn new ways, and the instructor has to reassure them that they really can learn the new operation. Once the employees want to learn, the instructor is in a good position to get them involved in the training and prepared to use specific methods that will be discussed later in this book.

QUESTIONS FOR SMALL GROUP DISCUSSIONS

1. List as many reasons why people learn as you can think of.

2. What is the smallest number of categories these reasons can be combined in?

3. What are some of the reasons you are reading this book? Do they fit into the categories you mentioned above?

4. What characteristics of poor salesmanship are sometimes present in our teaching efforts?

5. What are some of the ways we can "sell" training to the employee being trained?

6. What are some of the things supervisors can do to create enthusiasm in the people they are trying to teach?

7. How does the supervisor's attitude affect the learner's attitude? Give some examples.

8. What effect will a lack of proper background have on the employee's ability to learn? Give some examples.

9. What is meant by "rebellion against authority," and how does it affect training?

10. Give some examples of the difference between training that relates well to the job problems and training that fails to do this.

11. List the last five people you trained and discuss their reasons for learning and their attitude toward learning.

chapter 3

ON-THE-JOB TRAINING OR CLASSROOM TRAINING?

The question often arises as to *where* training should take place. Should a course be organized and a number of employees trained in a *classroom*, or should the employees be trained individually *on the job* by the supervisor? These are sometimes difficult questions to answer, but there are some guidelines that will help us.

There is a misconception that must be cleared up before we can compare the two methods. We must understand that there is *no perfect way to train in any specific case* where training is required. No one way is without its drawbacks. There are many considerations that present themselves. There are questions of money, time, effectiveness, energy required, instructors, and so forth. One method may be much more effective, but the cost may be prohibitive. Another may be cheap and effective but require more people or more time than is practicable. So it isn't just a matter of looking at classroom versus on-the-job training and saying that one is obviously better than the other. *Both have their good points and both have their drawbacks.*

SIMILARITIES BETWEEN ON-THE-JOB AND CLASSROOM TRAINING

We should see the similarities as well as the differences between the two methods in order to decide which would be best for a particular training program. For example, good communication is essential to all learning, no matter whether an employee is learning how to polish widgets, a schoolchild is learning fractions, or a preschooler is learning how to set the table. Someone who is good at communicating must show them how to do the job, or little learning will take place. Another similarity between classroom training and on-the-job training, at least in a company program, is that the instructor is very likely to be the employee's regular day-to-day supervisor as well. This double relationship can pose special problems of its own, and we should understand how to handle them before going on to decide where the training should take place. There are, of course, differences as well as similarities between on-the-job training and classroom training. We will discuss both the similarities and the differences in this chapter.

No matter what kind of training is done, *one basic requirement is good communication.* Whether there is a group of students in a classroom or one supervisor with one employee, the whole point of the relationship is for the teacher or supervisor to communicate information on certain skills. Even if the employee has only a textbook and no instructor at all, there still must be good communication. The book must be written so that the employee can easily grasp what is said, and it must present the information in such a way that the employee will not only be able to absorb the material, but be *motivated* to absorb it.

Good communication is not accidental. There are things that stand in the way of passing information to others, and there are things that aid the process. It doesn't matter if there is one employee or a dozen, they must hear words that are familiar and acceptable to them. If the idea of "company policy" waves a red flag in front of them, then constant reference to company policy as a reason for doing something is going to put up a roadblock to learning. An instructor who is down on unions and keeps referring to "those union thugs" is wasting time trying to train a group of union members. On the other hand, the instructor might be more accepted if she is willing to take a little kidding about the company or management. This doesn't mean that the instructor should purposely run down the company or the management; it just means that the instructor can let the kidding go without getting up on a stump and trying to defend every policy and decision that is attacked by the employees.

Of course, if it becomes obvious that these attitudes and feelings are so strong that training is hopeless, then it may be that a different kind of training is needed. Supervisors doing training should be careful not to try to change their course of instruction too much, though, because if they have done a good job of preplanning and setting objectives, they won't be prepared to teach something entirely different. They will have their goals set and their timing and other plans figured so closely that there won't be room or time for a whole new course.

Words Are Codes

The use of "unacceptable" words isn't the only roadblock to communicating. The use of words beyond the understanding of employees, because of their lack of education or experience, will produce the same poor results as unacceptable words. Instructors should realize that words are really just codes that we use to transmit ideas and thoughts. We take an idea that we want to give to someone else, and we put it into code. It travels from our brain to our mouth, where words are spoken, then passes through the air to the ear of the person we are trying to communicate with. Here it goes to the brain, where the code words are *decoded*. If we have said "red," the brain supplies a meaning for red because it has such a meaning stored. On the other hand, if we say "burple," nothing happens when the code gets to the other person's brain, because there is nothing stored that says what burple means.

The important thing to remember is that *we should always try to find words that the listener can decode.* We have to remember, too, that *the listener might not always decode exactly the same meaning we intended to put into the message.* Later we will talk about the importance of getting feedback, and here we see one of the big reasons why we need it. We need to find out just what the

listener is getting. If it doesn't match what we sent, then we have to adjust the message quickly and send another one, this time trying to find a different "code" that the listener will be able to translate into the proper meaning.

Since there is so much danger in coding and decoding ideas through the use of words, it would be more effective if we could find a way to communicate using only a limited number of words. This is not difficult to do if we spend a little time working on it before the training session. The first thing that comes to mind, of course, is the use of pictures. Obviously a picture can convey much more information and usually does it much quicker than words. It is difficult to describe a complex machine in words, but reasonably simple with one or more pictures. With a little artwork, parts of a machine can be made to stand out with color or with a cutaway view, something that would be impossible with words. Enlarged color photography can bring to life small parts that would be difficult to describe in words and very hard to see on the actual machine. With the use of transparencies, overlays can be made that show how a process or piece of equipment is put together. The overlays are added one at a time on top of each other as the process is explained. The pictures provide a means of instructing that is hard to beat. These methods produce good results whether used on the job or in a classroom, so here again there is a similarity between the two kinds of training.

Pictures aren't the only means we have of avoiding the use of words. Whether used on the job or with a group in a class-room, a well-constructed model of the thing being described is an excellent means of getting a message across. A *model* or *mock-up* can be carried right to the job site, with the advantage that *the real equipment does not have to be taken out of operation*. The model should look and "act" like the real thing for it to have the great-est value. It may be made smaller or larger than the real thing without too much difficulty, providing it is obvious to the employees being trained that there is a difference. The model is best used when the actual piece of equipment is not available. A good working model allows the employees to do hands-on training, which is usually the most practical and most effective way of learning outside of using the real thing. As we will see, the same steps are used when training on the model as on the actual equipment. *The idea of the model is to have something that is so similar to the working machinery that the employees can detect very little difference when they leave the model and go to the real thing.*

Ideally, the equipment actually used in production is the best substitute for words, because it is better than words, and better than pictures and models most of the time. It is usually available, though, only when the training is done on the job; hence the similarity between the two kinds of training breaks down. We will talk more about the advantages of using the real equipment a little later in this chapter.

Instructor–Employee Relationship

One more similarity between classroom and on-the-job training is the relationship that exists between the supervisor doing the training and the employee being trained. Earlier we discussed the fact that the person doing the training should accept the responsibility for the end product—the learning. This holds true regardless of where the training is done. On-the-job training brings the supervisor and the employee much closer together, but even in the classroom the instructor should try to get as close to a one-to-one relationship as possible. *Oddly enough, the problem in the classroom is that the instructor often fails to get a close enough relationship because of all the people, while on the job the instructor sometimes has trouble because of too close a situation caused by not enough people around.* The latter is much less of a problem, however, and almost always works toward better training.

The situation will usually determine the relationship that exists between the instructor and the employee. If the person who regularly supervises the employee is doing the training, it would be very difficult for the supervisor to try to become anything other than what he always is. Day-to-day relationships can't be discarded, and of course really shouldn't be. The supervisor should make every attempt to take advantage of such a relationship, *unless the relationship is undesirable. A person who is doing a poor job of supervising will have a pretty hard time overcoming this when training employees.* It may be that the same things that make a person a poor supervisor make a poor instructor. *Inability to communicate, lack of perception into employee problems, failure to accept the employee for what she is,* all of these things make not only a poor supervisor, but a poor instructor as well.

While it certainly shouldn't be taken as a rule, supervisors who discover that they are not successful as instructors may want to examine their position as supervisors. This may be a sign that they have some shortcomings, particularly if communication seems to be the trouble with the instructing. If the instructors find themselves saying over and over again, "But don't you remember, I *told* you . . . ," they probably have the answer to some of their supervisory troubles. If their efforts to communicate result in having to "tell" the same thing repeatedly, they are using a very poor method to pass information to their employees.

DIFFERENCES BETWEEN ON-THE-JOB AND CLASSROOM TRAINING

Just as there are similarities between training done on the job and that done in the classroom, there are some rather important differences. Remember, the reason for mentioning these likenesses and dissimilarities is to show that no one means is perfect, nor is one method always the best. Each has advantages and disadvantages. Supervisors should examine each of the methods and see what suits their needs and problems. (*In this book we are emphasizing on-the-job training, but not because it is the only method that should ever be used.*)

Communication

One major difference that works to the advantage of the person doing on-the-job training is that there is only one person to "*code*" ideas for. In the classroom the instructor must worry about trying to find words that can be *decoded* by the entire group, although each has a different background. When the supervisor is instructing one person on the job, the problems of communications are solved if the instructor can find the level that works for this one person.

Natural Environment

Another advantage of OJT is that the two participants are working in a *real* situation under nearly actual conditions, rather than trying to simulate them in the classroom. There is rarely ever a better arrangement than to have employees training at the machines where they normally work, especially if they actually train in the natural environment of the job. Such a situation cuts down considerably on the amount of information that has to be "transferred" from the training back to the job. This is one major problem with classroom training. It is always difficult to simulate a real situation in the classroom, so the employees find it equally difficult to make the application of the training when they get back to the job. On the other hand, when the training is done at the work site, they do not have to "carry" it back. So from this standpoint, on-the-job training has a decided advantage over classroom training.

Distractions

Anything that distracts the employees when they are trying to learn will interfere with communication, and hence prevent effective training. This is true regardless of where the training is conducted, but when the instructing is done at the job location, there is always a good possibility that there will be distractions from many sources. The presence of other workers, who may be naturally curious about what is going on, could distract from the learning process. The movement and noise of equipment, the conversations of other employees, the surroundings in general *all pose a hazard to the training effort.* Even though this is the natural setting for the job, and all of these distractions will be present when the employee will be doing the job, they still must be taken into consideration when the supervisor is trying to communicate with people on the job.

The presence of employees who are not involved in the training activity offers one of the biggest hazards, especially if they are allowed to stand around or make comments about what is going on. Their presence alone is enough to make the person being trained uneasy, and this uneasiness causes the employee to think more about their reactions than about the training that is going on. Such problems should be controlled, of course. If they continue, then the supervisor is not accepting the full responsibility of the job. Certainly the supervisor should not try to carry on the training while these things are going on.

This holds true for any kind of distraction. No training should be given when the conditions are all *against success.* It

isn't likely that there ever will be *perfect* conditions, but the supervisor should decide if the training has any real chance of being successful. If not, then the supervisor should wait for a better time or try to correct the poor condition. If the noise from the equipment is so loud or distracting that it seems unwise to try to conduct training, and it isn't possible to shut down the machinery, then there is no choice but to move to some other place and do the training. In this connection, there is something known as *vestibule training*, which simply means that the *training is done very close to the place where the work is going on, but not at the exact location because of noise, interruptions, etc.* The reason for having it close by is to try to create as nearly as possible the atmosphere of the job and perhaps to use some of the facilities that are found only at the job site. This is often a good compromise between the classroom and the actual job location.

Supervisor–Employee Relationship

Earlier we talked about instructor–employee relationships. It is difficult for employees to think of their supervisor as only an instructor, since they know this is the same person who is present all the time as their boss. For this reason, we need to talk about the problems that may arise as a result of such a feeling. We have already noted that the one-to-one ratio that exists when the training is done at the job location may put the supervisor in a slightly embarrassing position. It shouldn't, of course, but supervisors who haven't developed the right kind of atmosphere (and attitude) in their everyday dealings with their subordinates will find their training effort has many problems too. The important thing to remember—as we will see in more detail later—is that the employee must be put at ease before any of the training takes place. The supervisor cannot ignore the fact of being the boss, however, and the employee will know this from the beginning to the end of the training session. *The supervisor who doesn't try to put on an act of "aren't I the friendly fellow" will come out much better.* Employees will sense any effort by the boss as such a pretense, and when they spot this, they will be suspicious or confused, and not in the mood to learn.

Suppose the employee is very aware that this is the boss doing the training. What's so bad about this? Nothing is wrong with it. It's just that the instructor must realize that the employee is looking at the person who evaluates the job performance; the person who may be responsible for the employee's salary progress and possibly even promotions; the person who puts good and bad notations in the employee's personnel records; the boss who imposes restrictions and grants privileges. Hopefully the employee also sees the supervisor as the person who does a good job of training for the work that gets evaluated!

ADVANTAGES AND DISADVANTAGES OF ON-THE-JOB TRAINING

Let's summarize all of the advantages and disadvantages of using on-the-job training to make sure we see this type of instruction in its proper perspective. We'll look at the advantages first.

There is the matter of *time*. It generally is much quicker to train one person right at the job site than to bring the person into a formal classroom situation. There is less travel time to and from the training; it takes less preparation of facilities at the job site than in the classroom; the training can be more effective when done on the actual equipment, so time is saved through efficiency in training.

Next there is less *interference with production* because only one person is involved at a time. The supervisor can take the worker from the loom, or from the assembly line, or from whatever activity, and let the rest of the work go on. The training sessions are usually short anyway, so even if the employee is needed for production all the time, the shutdown time will be short.

Working under *actual conditions* has already been shown to be one very good advantage of training at the job location. We mention it again to emphasize that the whole point of training is to show the employee how to perform on the job. What better way to do this than to train under actual conditions, at the same place where the work is to be done, on the same equipment that is going to be used in doing the work?

Having the one person who knows the standard of a "good" job—the supervisor—do the training is certainly a major advan-

ADVANTAGES AND DISADVANTAGES

tage of on-the-job training. Taking employees off to a classroom has some advantages, but if the instructor in the classroom does not know exactly what is expected of the employees back on the job, practical training will not be accomplished. Even an instructor who has had considerable experience on the very job being trained for may still not know what exactly is expected of *this* employee, on this *specific* job, by this specific *boss*.

Finally there is the matter of *economics*. Having only one employee off the job at a time is less costly than taking several at the same time. If the production is not cut off, or at least is reduced only slightly, money is saved. The time saved by not having to move employees to a training room is always worth money. There is a saving, too, if it is not necessary to provide and maintain a classroom facility.

We have discussed some of the *disadvantages* earlier. Let's summarize them also.

The matter of the *supervisor representing authority can be a disadvantage*. The employee may resent being trained by the boss, especially if the boss exerts too much of this authority. ("Look, you'd better learn this in a hurry and get back to your job, or I'm going to dock your pay.")

One hindrance to any kind of instruction is a *poor trainer*. On the job the supervisor may be an excellent boss, he may know the job very well, and he may be well thought of by the employees, but teaching is a *skill* and the supervisor may not have this particular skill. If not, then it will be a drawback to good training. Some of the characteristics that make a person a good supervisor will help make a good instructor. *But one has to learn to be a good supervisor, so one must learn to be an instructor. To do otherwise will continue to be a "disadvantage" to on-the-job training.*

Distractions will interfere with successful training and are more likely to be present at the job site than elsewhere. The problem may be noise, other employees, people asking questions (of either the employee being trained or the person doing the training), normal movement in the surroundings, or a number of other things. Whatever they are, distractions are problems that have to be faced and solved before the training will be successful.

Time is also a disadvantage. While training one employee at a time is efficient for *that* employee, it certainly isn't the most efficient way to train large groups of people. If the supervisor is expected to carry a normal load and still spend considerable time training each employee individually, there is going to be a real time problem. Ideally, the time for training should be built into the job so that it can be taken as a regular part of the job and not sandwiched in between other assignments. In any case, it should be noted that good training takes time, and since good training is the only kind that will pay for itself, time (or lack of it) may be a disadvantage to doing the training on the job.

ADVANTAGES OF CLASSROOM COMBINED WITH OJT

Up to this point, it has sounded like there has to be a choice of doing the training either on the job one-on-one or in a classroom with several people. That's definitely not the case. There are things that can be done in the classroom, with models, cutaways, or examples, that cannot be done on the job. On the other hand, there are things that can be done on the job, where the actual work is being done in the true environment, that cannot be simulated in the classroom. For that reason, many organizations advocate doing both kinds of training, using each kind to its best advantage. Even on the job it is not necessary to do just one-on-one training: It may be getting three people around a machine and involved in doing the operation that's being taught. It is also helpful to get people in the classroom, where they can discuss flowcharts, graphs, purposes of certain kinds of equipment, certain kinds of procedures, and where safety, health, and environmental issues can be discussed without interruption from the actual noise and environment of the job.

CONCLUSION

There is no perfect way to train in any specific case where training is required. No one way is without its drawbacks. There are questions of money, time, effectiveness, energy required, instructors, and so forth. Supervisors should examine the advantages and disadvantages of each of the methods available and see what best suits their needs, problems, and situations.

In this book we're emphasizing on-the-job training. Some advantages we'll see are:

1. It generally is much quicker to train one person at the job site than to bring several people into a formal classroom situation.
2. There is less interference with production because only one person is involved in the training at a time.
3. Training under actual working conditions is nearly always more effective.
4. Having only one employee off the job at a time is less costly than taking several off together.

QUESTIONS FOR SMALL GROUP DISCUSSIONS

1. Is there a "perfect" way to train employees? Why or why not?

2. List some things that on-the-job and classroom training have in common.

3. What are some of the barriers to good communication?

4. Discuss the following incident from a training session: Two people, each active in union affairs, are being trained on a particular job by their supervisor. After the initial greetings, the supervisor breaks the ice by saying, "I don't have to tell you people that the contract doesn't provide for my doing this on such short notice, but the big boss has got a wild idea that we'd better be sure everybody knows this new technique. I'd appreciate it if you'd go along with me, so we can get it over with."

5. Explain the idea of "coding" and "decoding" in communicating with people.

6. What are some of the ways we can avoid the use of words in training?

7. Why do we avoid words sometimes in our training?

8. Is there any relationship between the success of a person as a supervisor and that person's success as an instructor? Discuss.

9. What are some of the differences between training done at the job site and training done in the classroom?

10. What problems may arise as a result of supervisors training the same people they supervise?

11. List the advantages of training done on the job over training done elsewhere.

12. What disadvantages are present when the training is done at the job location?

13. Discuss the advantages and disadvantages you listed in Questions 11 and 12 in relation to your own job, and see how many of each exist when you try to instruct your employees.

chapter 4

ANALYZING THE JOB TO BE DONE: I

WHAT IS A "GOOD" JOB?

The importance of answering the question of just what is a good job cannot be overemphasized. Only when we find the answer to this question are we able to determine how to rate an employee *now doing* the job and how to train an employee who is going to *start doing* the job. Of course, everybody has an answer to "What is a good job?" but the trouble is we don't always agree with each other. For instance, which of the following is a definition of a "good" job?

1. The employee does as much as the previous employees have done on the same job.
2. The employee does everything the supervisor expects to be done.
3. The employee does the job and always just a "little bit more."
4. The employee does less than the last person who was pro-

57

moted to a higher rated job, but more than the employee who was removed to a lower rated job because of "unsatisfactory work."

Let's take these definitions one at a time and see if they really tell us what a good job is. Number 1 tells us that the employee is doing the same amount as other employees have done but fails to tell us how good they were and what standard was used to measure them. We would not openly use this as a standard, but without knowing it we probably would use this one more than any of the others. "Charlie just doesn't do the work that Mary and Tom did before him. I'm going to have to do something to get his production up." Such a statement is not too unusual and shows we are using other employees to set the standard. Maybe we were spoiled by the other employees, or maybe they really weren't doing too well but had a supervisor who had set a lower standard than you have. The records show they were "satisfactory," but they never worked for you. Now you are in the job, and Charlie is working for you. You have your own definition of "satisfactory," and you assume that Mary and Tom must have been up to that standard if they were rated as they were. So in reality, *you* are setting the standard in this case.

This is what happens when we settle for number 2 as the measure of a "good" job. How often do we hear people commenting, "Jane sure does a good job. *She does everything I tell her to do and never complains.*" But is "everything I tell her" the job she is to be rated on? *Is it fair to her to let the supervisor set the standard, and that standard be so uncertain that it can be defined only as "everything I tell her to do"?* Suppose you were given the job of training the person who takes Jane's place. What kind of training would you give in this case? "Teach the basics," somebody says. All right, but are we going to hold the person accountable for more than the "basics" or just what we teach? "Sure, this job requires learning plenty more than the basics to do a good job." How much more? When will the employee have reached the point of doing "a good job"?

This leads us to number 3. "I can always depend on Max to do just that little extra amount on the job. He does his job all right, but then he is in there plugging for something else most of the time. If I can't find something to challenge him, he will spend the time finding better ways of doing the job. He has even had several employee suggestions accepted by the company." Now we are beginning to see the difference between a *good employee* and an employee doing a *good job*. There is a very distinct difference, and we should realize it before we start to train for any job. It's obvious that Max is doing his job well. But what makes Max stand out is that he is constantly finding better ways of doing a job. We should not keep him from improving the job by simply giving him more work to do. If we're going to train him, we would do better to train him in ways of recognizing inefficiency and poor procedures on the job, rather than to do just more of the same kind of work. A good employee can be defined as an employee who is not only doing a good job up to standards, but is also constantly looking for ways of improving whatever job is being done. The fact that Max has actually had his suggestions accepted, whether by a committee or by some program the organization has, shows that he is indeed a good employee.

Number 4 brings this out more clearly. Here we have an employee who does less than the person who was promoted but more than the one who was removed from the job. If Max is as good as he seems, then he probably should be promoted. The things he is doing are what we look for when we have a job that is higher rated and want to fill it from the ranks of those at a lower level. We ask ourselves, "which employee is capable of handling more than he is handling right now?" Max's name should come to the forefront. But remember, we thought of his name not just because he is doing a good job, but because he has demonstrated the ability to do *more* than what is required on his present job. If Max is promoted, then we have to watch ourselves to be sure not to set him up as the standard for the person taking his job. We have been happy with Max. He has done the job and *more*. It would be nice if we could find someone just like Max to fill the job. But do we *need* another Max to do the work satisfactorily? When we set the objectives for our training, are we going to say that the employee will be able to do the job plus something extra, then train the employee on these extras as well? If not, then we haven't found the definition of a good job yet!

But we have to know what a good job is in order to train the employees. There isn't any mystery about it, but we mentioned

these examples because we get caught in a trap occasionally by letting the supervisor set the standard without actually being able to define it very well. *Suppose we had had a number 5 which said that "A good job is done when the employee matches up with a detailed job analysis, written in terms of what will be expected on the job."* Now can we measure the employee? We can if the job analysis has such expressions as, "The employee will be able to turn out 100 items a day with no more than 5 that do not pass inspection," or "The employee will be able to locate any troubles in the following list of small appliances," or "The employee will compute and check–balance accruals at the end of each day. The books will balance each day with all monies accounted for."

With these standards it is easy to determine if the employee is doing a good job. We look at the job description and then at the employee. Is the employee turning out 100 items a day with 95 percent accuracy? Is the employee able to locate all troubles in the following list of small appliances? Can the employee balance the books at the end of each day, at the same time accounting for all monies? *Look how easy the training becomes when we have a standard like this.* We know exactly what is expected of the employee, so we know exactly what to train for and what to measure for when we evaluate the training. We have also eliminated a lot of guess work in finding the standard. Neither the supervisor nor the other employees have set the standard.

We recognize that sometimes it is difficult to set standards. Take the example of trouble-shooting. Initially the experienced employee who has seen a lot of troubles, who has experimented and has found trouble, is more likely to be good at trouble-shooting than an inexperienced employee, or an employee new on a particular job. Some troubles are located simply by gut feeling, but we can't train people to have gut feelings. If we expect trouble-shooting to be a part of the job's entry-level assignment, then we have to be able to define and train on trouble-shooting. It may well be that we'll limit the trouble-shooting to some minimum activities and define those, such as "being able to determine why the belt is not turning or why the power is not reaching a certain part of the equipment, or explaining the options when a piece of equipment is automatically shutting itself down." However we define it, it has to be measurable and observable and you have to be able to train the person on how to do it.

But we shouldn't think that this takes away the prerogatives of the supervisor to judge the employee's performance. We have plenty of room for judgment. What we have done is to give the supervisor a standard that is real and *stable* in that it does not vary from one supervisor to the next, nor change when one employee is promoted or removed from the job. It gives a realistic means of determining what kind of training is required. Just as important, it gives the employees a clear target to shoot at. They know how well they are doing because they know the standard. They know how far they have to go to learn the job and have a good reason for taking training. There is a point of reference between the employee and the supervisor when it comes time to do the training. The supervisor can say, "Joan, as you know, the requirements for this job are . . . ." If Joan isn't meeting these standards, she should be glad to have some training that will help get her up to satisfactory performance.

WHY NOT SATISFACTORY PERFORMANCE?

In a little while we will talk in more detail about analyzing a job to set the standard, but for now let's assume we have such a standard. We should know why it is that some employees do not measure up. Here are some of the reasons why employees do not do a satisfactory job:

- Bad attitude
- Need training
- Don't know what they are supposed to do
- Lack of ability
- Poor job organization
- Unsupportive work environment
- Lack of performance feedback

Any of these, or a combination, is reason enough for the employee to be performing unsatisfactorily. Look more closely, though, and see that almost any of these could either *cause* or *be caused by any other one.* What we should do is try to find out when training is the problem and when it isn't. We want to know when training will *solve* the problem, and when it will not. It is dangerous to think that training will solve all problems of poor performance.

For instance, let's look at "bad attitude." *Perhaps nothing is more obvious about an employee, yet more difficult to explain, than good and bad attitudes.* Since attitudes have been the subject of entire books, we will look at them only as they influence training.

The important thing is to determine whether training will improve the attitude. If the employees know what is expected of them, have had proper training, and have done the job correctly in the past, but have begun to perform incorrectly lately, the chances are training will not help. On the other hand, if the employees are confused and not sure what is expected of them, or if they have never performed satisfactorily even though they seem to have the capabilities, then there may be a training problem.

One of the advantages of having a good job description is to eliminate some of the errors that get into our decisions over the matter of attitudes. It is easy to mark employees down by saying they have a bad attitude, but when there is a specific standard of work performance to go by, it is not as easy. If we have to identify the particular part of the job description that is not being carried out, we are more likely to look at job functions than attitudes. The point is, of course, that job functions are measurable; attitudes are not. We need to be prepared to defend our position when we confront an employee with a statement like, "Buck, your job is all right, but I don't like your attitude." Unless we mean that Buck's attitude is hindering others from doing their jobs, we may have a hard time explaining to him that he's actually meeting the standards of the job but we'd like to have him smile a little more around the shop. (It would be even more difficult to answer him if he asked, "Why don't you *train* me to smile?") Bad attitudes may indicate a need for training, but there should be more evidence than just the supervisor's opinion that training will help.

WILL TRAINING HELP?

When an employee is not doing the job satisfactorily, it is often assumed that there is a need for training. This may be the case and training may help, but we need more evidence than just an unsatisfactory job. There are reasons why employees fail in their job other than the lack of training. For example, the person may not have an aptitude for doing the work. An employee who has been trained and has been working on the job for some time has an "attitude" of wanting to do a good job. In spite of all this, the job is still being done in a substandard way. If the training was really effective and the employee still can't do the job (even though she's trying hard), then we should not expect to do more training until we decide if the employee has the ability to do this particular work assignment.

On the other hand, there are some cases where training is obviously the answer. If the employee is new on the job or the job has changed and there has been no training (and the job is being done unsatisfactorily), then training should be the first order of business. It is not very practical to put a new employee on a job or put a new piece of equipment in front of an experienced person, but then not do the training that is required. It is equally dangerous to put off the training or schedule it "when it is convenient."

Another reason we listed as why employees don't do their jobs properly is that they don't know what they are supposed to do. Is training the answer in this case? It depends on how much there is to tell them about what they are supposed to do. *If they don't know what their responsibility is*, then it may just be a matter of telling or showing them one time and that's all. It may be that George is to put the final polish on an item, but he was under the impression that somebody else did that after the item left him. His own effort was just a slight brush for good measure. In this case, just a word should be sufficient. But suppose the final

WHY ISN'T HE DOING THE JOB CORRECTLY?

polishing takes a particular kind of hand movement with the polisher to get the sheen required. Now we have a small training situation. So the end product—an unpolished item—was the same, even though the cause for the bad result was different. In both cases, the responsibility is in the hands of the supervisor to correct.

What about the lack of ability? This will certainly cause employees to perform poorly on the job. But are we sure the employee doesn't have the ability? Are we able to look at a worker and say, "There's a person who just doesn't have it"? It would be nice if we could, but unfortunately that isn't a very good test of ability. Then maybe we can look at the person's *work* and draw some conclusion. Suzie is a drafting clerk with a large number of incorrect strokes that almost anyone who has been doing drafting work as long as she has should know how to do properly. Can we conclude she just doesn't have the ability to make the proper stokes? Not unless we are sure she has had adequate training. All right, suppose we check the record and find she not only had the training but came through it with an adequate rating, indicating she was at one time capable of doing a satisfactory job.

Now we have eliminated one possible cause but have found another. It would seem that we now have an attitude problem. But wait, maybe not. There is plenty of evidence to show that *employees forget some of the things they learn*, especially when there is no particular emphasis put on them over a long period. *It may be that as time has gone by, the supervisor has allowed poor quality of work to get by without trying to correct it.* When something is finally said, it is because the work has gotten so bad there is a complaint at higher levels or in other departments. The supervisor really takes a critical look at the work, realizes it is very bad, and blames it on the drafting clerk. The supervisor may express this in a number of ways. "Suzie sure has got a bad attitude. She just lets her work get so sloppy, the whole drafting department gets a bad name," or the supervisor may not have been around very long and so seeks to put the blame on someone else. "Somebody just failed to get rid of her. She was this way when I got here." The supervisor may say the same thing in another way. "Suzie just hasn't got it. I've been her supervisor for eight months, and she has yet to do a decent job."

One can't help but want to ask a number of questions of the supervisors who make those kinds of statements: *"What have you done to correct the poor quality of work? Does Suzie know how bad you think her work is? Have you shown her the proper way to do her work?* Have you suggested a training program for her? Do you have her training record to show that she has or hasn't had a chance to learn how to improve her work?" (And maybe a few more that you can think of.)

Another possible reason for poor performance is poor job organization. Let's look at a job that consists of packing certain pieces of heavy equipment that come off the end of the line. The equipment is too heavy to lift easily but can be moved by Stan with a dolly under it. It comes to him already on the dolly. He is to position it in front of the bin where the bolts are kept. After mounting the legs with large bolts, Stan is supposed to position and bolt large angle-iron braces crisscross on the side opposite from the bin. This requires carrying the heavy braces around the equipment, then coming back to the bin for the mounting bolts. Sixteen bolts are required, which Stan is to carry in his hand. After the first eight are in place, the equipment is considered secure enough that the dolly can be removed for use on the next piece of equipment coming along the line. The piece Stan is working on is lifted by a motorized lift while the dolly is removed, then placed on the floor for completion. When the final bolts are in place, the lift carries the equipment to the next station for boxing.

The problem arises when extra bolts are sometimes discovered on the floor, and random inspection shows that some of the bolts are left out of the crisscross mountings. The first conclusion is that Stan is doing a careless job, failing to put in all of the bolts. This would account for the bolts on the floor and the ones missing from the finished product. Stan has a different story when finally confronted with the problem. "Counting out sixteen bolts, then carrying them around the equipment just doesn't make any sense, especially after carrying the heavy braces, too. What happens is that sometimes I get to the last bolt and discover I've got two more holes or *no more holes*. Since the braces are strong enough after eight bolts to lift from the dolly, I don't figure leaving one out is going to hurt anything. When I have one bolt left over, I either have to carry it all the way back to the bin or leave it on the floor. Sometimes I just forget it's there and get sixteen more on the next operation. Besides, I don't see why the equipment can't be left turned toward the bin so I don't have to carry all the braces and bolts."

Stan's point is well taken. If we concluded that Stan just didn't know how to do his job and decided to give him training, we would be wasting his time and ours. Maybe Stan is sloppy in his work, but it looks as if others were just as sloppy in their planning when they set up the major work operation away from the storage bin. There may be a good reason, though, or it may be that it's too late to make a change in the operation. If so, then training may be needed, but not the kind we first thought of. We may have to give Stan a safety course to show him the danger in leaving foreign objects on the work floor. We may have to show him a little about stress and strain in shipping equipment in order for him to see the importance of having all the bolts in place when the equipment is actually handled in shipment. Above all, it isn't enough to just write Stan off as a poor employee, or to give him a refresher course in putting sixteen bolts in a piece of equipment!

Someone has suggested that one test that we can make on whether an employee needs training, whether he has a bad attitude, or whether it is something about the job that prevents the job being done properly is to ask ourselves, "If I put a gun to the person's head and said, 'do the job or I will shoot,' would they and could they do the job?" Although this is a figurative example, the point is simply being made that we don't want to train someone if she already knows how to do the job. On the other hand, we *must* train somebody who doesn't know how to do the job.

WHAT ABOUT EMPLOYEES ALREADY TRAINED?

One way to determine the need for training is to look at what the employees who have already been trained are doing. Here is a good way to decide whether what we think is a "good job" is really accurate or not. At least we can see what the probable result of training will be. Those who have been trained are now able to do it this way; if we train someone else with equal ability and desire, that person should be able to perform the same way. The question we have to answer is, "Will we be satisfied with this kind of performance?" If not, then we will have to find a better way to produce the result we want, for example, by getting someone with more experience or talent, or by changing the training.

If those employees who are now on the job are rated as doing a satisfactory job and have had the training, then we should be satisfied with the training *even though we do not like the way the training is done, nor the material that is covered.* As we begin to analyze the performance of the already trained people, we are getting close to analyzing the job. Sooner or later we will have to do just that. But along the way, we are doing something else: We are doing an *employee work analysis. Finding out what is actually done by existing employees will help us best determine just what we should really expect on the job.* It will help us decide if the job is organized wrong, if the present work requirements are too much or too little, if the present training methods are producing properly trained employees, and perhaps much more information.

CONCLUSION

What is a "good job"? Only when we find the answer to this question can we determine how to rate an employee now doing the job and decide how to train an employee who is going to start doing the job. A "good" job is done when the employee matches up with a detailed job description, written in terms of what will be expected. We can measure the employee doing the job, if the job description has expressions such as, "The employee will be able to run out 100 items an hour, with no more than five that do not pass inspection," or "The employee will be able to locate the trouble in any of the following small appliances within ten minutes of beginning the trouble-shooting." With these standards it is easy to determine if the employee is doing a *good* job. We look at the job description and then look at the employee's performance to see if they match. We know exactly what is expected of the employee so we know exactly what to train for and what to measure when we evaluate the training.

QUESTIONS FOR SMALL GROUP DISCUSSIONS

1. A supervisor rates an employee as follows: "Margie isn't doing as good a job as she could. The three people who had the job before her could turn out 125 units a day, but Margie's best effort is a consistent 110 units." How good is this as a measure of whether or not Margie is doing an acceptable job?

2. Discuss this incident that took place between the foreman and one of his men: "Frankly, Chuck, you just aren't measuring up. If you expect to get ahead around here, you are going to have to put out a little extra effort as Frank did. He got promoted for always giving it that little bit more."

3. Your job is to develop a training program for four file clerks in the office, and you are looking for a standard to go by. The boss shows you the records of the clerks, and you see that one is rated as *above average*, one is *below average*, and the other two are rated as *satisfactory*. How will you determine the standard for an acceptable job when you develop your training program?

4. Discuss the case of Buck mentioned in this chapter. ("Buck, your job is all right, but I don't like your attitude.") Should Buck receive training, and if so, what kind? What will you tell Buck when you start the training program?

5. Pick an employee you have who you think has a poor attitude. Discuss the reasons why you say this employee has this attitude. How is the work affected? How can training help her?

chapter 5

ANALYZING THE JOB
TO BE DONE: II

Let's see how to analyze an employee's work. Remember, we are looking at the *employee's actual work*, not the job we think the employee should be doing. What about the case of the drafting clerk who was turning in sloppy work? What about Stan and the bolts? What about George, who fails to polish the item properly before it goes to the next station? Let's look at how we would analyze their work and see if we couldn't have helped them before they got into trouble.

In the case of failing to put the finishing polish on the item, the analysis would have been fairly simple. George takes the item from the finishing mold, smooths the rough edges, measures it for tolerance, runs the burnisher over it lightly, and places it on the belt. To get the best information we can, *we should watch him do several in a row, or one every few minutes*. In other words, get a look at a proper sampling of his work before deciding for sure that what we have seen really represents his work. We would do well to write down the steps in each operation so we can see if he does the same thing every time. To get the real picture, we should even record it by hand movements. The analysis might look as shown in the accompanying work analysis (see Figure 5.1).

Figure 5.1   Work Analysis

Step	Work Operation
1	Removes item from mold with left hand; places it on work area slightly to right of center.
2	Lifts item with right hand; visually inspects it by turning it around completely; sets it down in same spot.
3	Lifts item with left hand; grasps polisher with right hand. Rotating item with left hand, removes rough edges with polisher in right hand. Replaces polisher and sets item down to left of center.
4	Picks up preset micrometer from left-hand drawer with left hand; passes it to right hand; picks up item with left hand.
5	Passes micrometer around all parts to be measured for tolerance; sets item down left center; passes micrometer to left hand and replaces it in original drawer.
6	Picks up item with left hand, polisher with right hand, and gives entire item one pass with polisher; sets item down left center; replaces polisher.
7	Picks up item with left hand; visually inspects it by turning it around.
8	Places item on belt with right hand.

Looking closely at this analysis, we find a number of things that suggest the need for training, and some that may call for a change in organization. Go back over the analysis and check the things that appear to be wrong.

Let's assume that time is a problem. If so, then every little bit of motion that is saved is time that can be recovered. (For instance, if we save 20 seconds on an operation that is repeated 200 times a day, then we have saved more than an hour of production time.) We see in step 1 that George lifts the item with the *left* hand and sets it down *right* center so it will be in the correct position for step 2. In step 2, he picks it up with his *right* hand to inspect it visually. Positioning it in right center in step 1 seems to be a good idea, except that when we analyze it more carefully, we see that a whole step could have been saved if he had picked it up with his *right* hand from the line to *start with*. He could have done his visual inspection in this one step, and not set it down until he was ready to change hands. But now note that in step 2, he set it down in *right* center but had to pick it up with his *left* hand, meaning he had to reach across to pick it up. Had he set it down *left* center this extra motion could have been saved.

But now let's go back to step 1 and the *left* hand. In step 3 he shifts it back to his left hand so he can hold the polisher with the right hand. This means that he will be able to rotate it for polishing with the left hand, so why not rotate if for inspection with the left hand? Then we can eliminate another step because the item can be kept in the left hand all the time. Now all he has to do is lift it from the mold with his left hand, turn it for inspection, pick up the polisher with his right hand, and burnish the rough spots.

In steps 4 and 5 we see an obvious organization and storage problem. Everything has to stop while George gets the micrometer from the *left*-hand drawer. At the end of the polishing operation, the same thing happens. The item is set down while George puts back the micrometer in the drawer. Two questions should come to mind: Why have it on the *left* side and why have it in a *drawer* at all? The micrometer is a vital part of the operation and is used on every piece that is taken from the line. Even though the micrometer may be delicate, chances are good that a place could be found for it on the work area that would still protect it from being knocked off or struck in some way. The work operation could then be simplified considerably. If we made these changes, the job analysis would look as shown in Figure 5.2. (Remember we are now talking about how the *job should look*, so this is a job analysis chart rather than an analysis of the actual work operation.)

There may be other ways of changing this procedure, but note that the operation is much smoother now and should go faster. There may be a question of fatigue if the item is too heavy, since it is held in the left hand the entire time without setting it down. The supervisor can tell this without much trouble, though, and since this isn't a lengthy operation, fatigue shouldn't be a problem.

The advantage of this exercise is that if we had gone into the first operation and done our training, we wouldn't have improved the organization of the job, only the work itself. The rea-

Figure 5.2   Job Analysis Chart

Step	Job Operation
1	Removes item from mold with left hand; visually inspects it by rotating it completely.
2	Picks up polisher with right hand and removes rough edges; replaces polisher with right hand and picks up micrometer with same hand.
3	Passes micrometer around all parts to be measured for tolerance; replaces micrometer on bench; picks up polisher with same hand motion.
4	Does finishing job with polisher by using circular motions with right hand; replaces polisher.
5	Rotates items in left hand for inspection; places it on the belt with the same hand.

son we were even looking at the work to begin with was that the employee was failing to give á finished polish job. When we analyzed the entire operation, we discovered some things even more significant than the polishing.

We saved time and work energy. Now when we train we have a different problem because we have to change the entire operation, not just the polishing part. But we have a good step-by-step chart to go by. As we will see later, this is essential to any successful on-the-job training activity.

We won't go into as much detail on the other jobs, but let's look for a moment at the drafting clerk's performance. Suppose we make a partial work analysis sheet on how Suzie *receives and distributes* her work. This does not consider the position of instruments, the manner of storing the equipment, or the way she holds the pencil. *It looks at the work flow rather than the work performance.* The reason for this is to see if there is something about the manner in which work comes and goes to her desk that would interfere with her doing a proper job.

Let's assume that the operation requires the engineer to make field notes and then bring them in for Suzie to produce the final construction drawings. She also uses the specification books and prices out the job, entering the figures in a form that is provided. The engineer must sign the finished job as correct, so it goes to the engineer before it is passed to the supervisor for final approval and acceptance. We analyze the work flow as shown in Figure 5.3.

There would be more to the analysis if we included what happens if the supervisor finds errors and where the other engineers fit into the picture with their corrections, but we will not go that far. The supervisor *should* do the whole analysis, however, to get a true picture of the training and reorganization that may be required.

Now what have we found out in this flow analysis? (Again we suggest you go through and make any notes of questionable areas.) The first thing that should bother us is that Suzie gets work from three different engineers who have no say as to when the work will be done. Also, she takes *oral* notations from them although she may not get around to their work until after she has worked on other jobs and had a chance to forget the instructions. How are we going to train her to remember these notes?

Figure 5.3   Work Flow Sheet

Step	Work Operation
1	Engineer gives field notes to drafting clerk with written and oral notations. (She accepts work from three engineers on a "first come, first served" basis unless otherwise ordered by her supervisor.)
2	She is free to decide whether to find the specifications and pricing information now or wait until she starts to work on that particular job. She may work on more than one job at a time if she likes. When she is working on a job, she must have the specifications at hand at all times. She gets these from files across the room.
3	When the drawings are completed and the pricing done, she passes the finished drawings back to the engineer.
4	The engineer checks the drawings as time is available, then returns the drawings to her for correction. She makes notations on a ruled pad as the engineer shows her the necessary changes and uses this as a checklist for corrections.
5	The drafting clerk makes the requested changes and returns the drawing to the engineer. The process is repeated until the engineer is satisfied that the drawings are correct, then the engineer signs them and passes them to the supervisor.

How are we going to train her to determine which drawings get priority instead of a "first come, first served" treatment? Do we want to train her on these things? Of course, each job is separate, and we would have to know more about the people and the problems before we could reorganize the job, but we would have to solve some of these problems before we could begin to train.

One possibility would be for the supervisor (or "project director") to assign a priority number to each job, thus eliminating the need for any decision on her part or any haggling by the engineers. She should not be put in a situation where her decisions will cause conflict among the engineers. If there is something about the completion target date of the final construction that will give her specific enough information to assign priority to the job, then the problem is less difficult. We have only to train her to recognize the significance of the dates, and the problem is solved.

The matter of oral instructions comes up in step 4 also, so let's look at that problem. If she tries to remember what is said, she will almost certainly forget something at one time or another. If the engineer writes down the instructions, at least all of the information will be there for her to use when she gets to the job. But there is a chance she will misunderstand the written instructions, even if the engineer explains them to her. She—in listening and reading—has not become involved in the note making. She has just listened to the way the engineer explained the things to be done. A possible improvement would be to let her make her own notes as the engineer explains the job. She writes down the things the engineer wants added or changed as the engineer talks and points to the drawing or field notes. When the engineer is through, she then goes over her notes one by one and tells the engineer how she understands what has been said. This way she is very much involved and will remember what *she* said much longer than what the engineer said to her. (When we get to Chapter 8 on how to do the actual training, we will see that this idea fits very well the principle we will be using.) This is something we can train her to do and give her plenty of practice in making notes of her own. In the long run, this method will not take any more time, and the end result should be much more accurate.

The second thing we notice about our work flow analysis is that Suzie has no particular order of doing things when it comes to gathering the backup information she will need when she starts to work on a specific job. She gets the specifications and pricing information at any time she wants. This is hard to train her on since there is no specific procedure. Apparently there is no good reason not to get it as soon as she is given the job, but it may be that the time required would interfere with a drawing she is on right now. Also, if she is assigning time to the jobs, breaking away from one job to another may result in time charge errors. Perhaps as we look at the work operation, we will find that the best thing is for her to gather the reference materials at the time she is ready to go to work on that project. If so, then the training job will be simplified because it makes a neater package having all of the work done from beginning to end without stopping.

What about all the instructions she received from the engineer? That was some time ago, so the job really isn't being done in one package after all. *But why not?* The engineer could wait to give specific instructions until she is ready to start on the whole job. Now we have the job organized efficiently and are in a much better position to train. *If we had not gone through the work flow analysis, we might have just started training in the way she was already doing the job and failed to improve the work flow.* Note that we still haven't improved her poor drafting work, which was the thing that called our attention to her in the first place. But we may have helped the problem considerably by getting things organized and calling attention to the fact that we wanted things to be done less haphazardly. The matter of improving her drafting skill has taken a different light now that we have seen the problem from a larger viewpoint. When we start to work on her drafting, we may well want to break it down the same way. This time we would look for much smaller work units, including her manner of placing the field notes, the slant of the pencil, and the way she holds the drawing instruments.

We have already discussed the case of the employee bolting equipment for shipping, so we won't go into this much further. Note how we would have solved the problem if we had made a work analysis chart on him We would have seen that he was spending far too much time and energy walking around the job site carrying braces and bolts. When we had finished, we would have seen right away that we would want to avoid training the employee to do the job the way he was doing it now. It didn't make any sense to him to do it the way he was doing it; after making an analysis, *it probably wouldn't have made much sense to us either*!

How does it happen that work operations get disorganized like these we have been looking at? Don't people know better,

and can't they see that there are better ways of doing the job? Sure they can, but let's remember that very few jobs just *happen*, that is, just come into being overnight. *Usually jobs evolve.* At one time they were organized correctly and efficiently, but then the work or equipment was changed slightly. If it wasn't much of a change, then probably it didn't affect the work enough to bother with reorganization. Probably, too, the training was not updated, so the employees continued to be trained in what they had been doing. If the training was changed, it was probably changed only for that small part of the job that was affected and not for the total work operation. Gradually the job evolved into something quite different from what it was originally, but by now it is not being done very efficiently or effectively. This is where the supervisor comes into the picture. Supervisors need to see the *whole* job, not just the parts. They may train in parts, as we will see later, but all the training should fit into the total work operation. When they are analyzing jobs, they are doing it for more than training purposes. They are doing it to see if there is a *better way to get the job done.*

ANALYZING THE JOB

Up until now we have been talking about analyzing a job *while we watch the employee do the job.* This is helpful because it allows us to improve on the performance of someone doing the work by watching it being done, then deciding if there is a better way of doing it. This also allows us to see if we can find the cause of low production: Is it the employee or the job? But we can't do very much training and shouldn't do much appraising if this is all we use to go on. *There must be a standard to go by that tells not only what is to be done but how well it is to be done.* In Chapter 8 we deal with "how" to do the job, but we are talking about *a standard for how much, how well, and how often.* (In the next chapter, we will talk about setting objectives for training, and what we are talking about right now will help us understand what is said in that chapter.)

Let's look at the information in Figure 5.2 again. Notice that there are no standards for doing the various operations. We were not interested in standards when we made that chart. We wanted to know the step-by-step procedures in getting the job done. We were interested in quality only so far as *job design* was concerned. We were interested to see if the right steps were being taken in the right order. That's all we could appraise, by the way, from this information. We could not use that chart alone and give the employee a "good" or "bad" rating. If the order was wrong, and we had trained the employee in the correct method, or warned the employee that the job was being done incorrectly, then we could appraise this, but not the quality of performing these tasks! Why? Because we have failed so far to state the quality we are looking for. We do that by setting up another column, as shown in Figure 5.4.

We now add the matter of quality to the analysis. We still have the column for "action," but now there is one for the *"standard."* Remember, this is a "how well, how much, how often" kind of thing. It has to be *observable* and *measurable.* We also have reduced the amount of wording under "action" because now we want only the specific action, not anything that comes close to being a standard. For example, just saying that the item is lifted from the mold "with the left hand" is giving some standard to the action. Notice that under "standard" we have included the left-hand requirement. One of the questions we should ask about what goes in this column is, "Does it make any difference how it's done?" If doing it with the right hand is just as satisfactory, then *nothing* goes in this column about which hand to use.

Figure 5.4—Job Analysis Chart

Step	Action	Standard
1	a) Remove item from mold	a) With left hand. With continuous motion. End up with elbow bent at approximate right angles, forearm vertical.
	b) Visually inspect item.	b) Rotate complete turn horizontally. Lower arm to where all of top surface is visually inspected. Note (visually) protrusions, indentations, cracks. Complete inspection within 20 seconds of lifting from line.

Notice, too, that we put some other things in the "standard" column. We give observable measurements as to rotating the item being inspected, specific things to be observed, and a time limit. If it doesn't matter how the job is done, or even how a part of the job is done, then it doesn't go in this column. At the same time, if it does matter and the employee is expected to do it, it should be in this column. For example, if the inspection is supposed to include any discolorations, this standard does not allow for it. On the other hand, it frees the inspector from the obligation of worrying about the color. If the inspection shows that there is a very bad color streak right through the middle of the item, according to this standard, nothing would be thought about it. There is nothing to require the inspector to notice it or mention it or correct it. It's not enough to say, "Well they ought to know that we can't accept one that looks like that!" Another important consideration is that we have no right to find fault with the employee who does not find and correct the discoloration. At appraisal time, we're way off base when we say that a certain employee is not doing a satisfactory job because she is missing the discoloration. It's very simple: If an employee is going to be appraised on an operation, we ought to be able to write down the standards.

Of course, we're talking about training, not evaluation. It's hard to separate the two, however, since we have to have a standard before we can do either one successfully. Sometimes we get to thinking that a standard is something mysterious. Perhaps it would help us to think about appraisals as we think of standards, instead of in terms of training. It is always difficult, for some reason, to think of training in a direct relationship with the job. It remains something separate and apart from the job, instead of the thing that makes the job go. If this is a problem with us, then we should simply ask ourselves, "What kind of performance will we be satisfied with?" When we put the answer down, we should have a pretty good standard to go by. Too often we find ourselves getting a "job description" mixed up with the standard. More and more, job descriptions are getting longer and more "performance" oriented. This is too bad, because what we need is a job description *and* a job analysis. *The job description simply gives the areas of responsibility, while the job analysis gets down to the standards by which these responsibilities are to be carried out.* There are other things, such as the "Procedures Manual," that get involved in talking about the job, and different people write them in different ways. The procedures manual most often gets into the *how-tos* rather than *how much*, and rarely gets into the *whys* of doing a job a certain way.

Let's think about standards for a few jobs. For example, suppose we were going to train someone to write collection letters. We won't go into all the details, but we'll list some examples of what we mean about standards for different jobs. Under "standard" we might have things like "Two paragraphs" or "No more than 200 words" or "Informal block" or "Ask for the money in both paragraphs." Any or all of these represent measurable standards. The standard for balancing books would be "Accounting for all monies with no error," while for a store clerk it might be, "With no more than 2% error average, and no more than six errors in one sales day." For a typist, "No corrections in date, address, greeting, and first paragraph." Each step is treated the same way until the entire job operation is completely covered.

One final word—don't overlook a good source of help in analyzing the job, especially if you are looking for ways of simplifying it: the employee now doing the job. It's hard to imagine an employee who hasn't found a better way of doing a job. If we can get the employee to help us in doing the analyses we need to do, we may get a much better result. The employee may have a number of good ideas that would improve work flow, produce better results on the job, and save some time in the process. Just let the employee know you're genuinely interested in the ideas; even let the ideas be submitted in writing. Most employees are looking for ways to simplify their own jobs, so they are usually glad to spend some time in saying how it should be done. There is another important benefit for you in letting the employees get involved in helping set standards: Some of the training can be eliminated since they'll see much of what they need to know as they construct the analyses.

CONCLUSION

We should first analyze the employee's actual work. A good step-by-step chart of the work being done is essential to any successful on-the-job training activity. This requires observing the employees as they work. As we observe the performance of the person doing the job, we can also decide if there is a better way of doing it. We also need more than this. There must be a standard to go by that tells not only what should be done but also how well it should be done. We need both a *job description* and a *job analysis*. The job description simply gives the areas of responsibility, while the job analysis gets down to the standards by which these responsibilities are to be carried out. As supervisors do the analysis, they should not overlook a good source of help in looking at the actual procedures of the job: the employee now doing the job. If we can get the employee to help do the analysis, we may get better results in both the job and the training for the job.

QUESTIONS FOR SMALL GROUP DISCUSSIONS

1. Discuss ways of determining if poor performance by an employee is the result of a poor attitude, lack of training, or lack of ability.

2. Watch someone do a small task and then analyze it. (This may be sharpening a pencil, getting silverware and napkins on a tray at lunchtime, or stapling papers together.) Make up a chart on the operation and see if the work could have been done more efficiently or quickly. Now make up a job analysis chart on how you think the job could be done better. (Remember to break it down small enough to show the reasons for each step.)

3. Pick one of the jobs done by one of your employees and make a job analysis chart on it. Do this without watching the employee work. Now watch the employee and make a work analysis sheet on performance and compare the two.

chapter 6

DETERMINING OBJECTIVES

So far we have talked about reasons for training and reasons for not training. We have talked about the advantages and disadvantages of training in the classroom and on the job. We have looked at the supervisor as the instructor and seen the good and bad features of the supervisor doing the training. We've discussed how to get realistic looks at both the employee and the job by doing a work analysis chart (looking at how the job was *actually* being done by a specific employee) and a job analysis chart (stating how the job *should* be done, step by step). Now *let's talk about the things we have to do in preparing for the actual training.* Of course, the *job analysis* is a necessary function, and it should be done even when training isn't under consideration. It should be on hand as a means to measure employees' day-to-day performance and to discuss any shortcomings they may have. *It must be available when the training starts.*

WHY OBJECTIVES?

When we start our training, we need to have some *target* to shoot at, some *aim* in mind to tell us if we have been successful. We will call this our *objective*. We are going to set up some specific rules for *preparing* the objectives and for determining when they have been met. We will give some examples—both good and bad—and try to see how we can use the things we have already learned to improve our ability to prepare good objectives. *The single most important measurement of whether our training is going to be successful is our ability to properly state our objectives.*

Why are objectives so important? After all, isn't an objective just the "purpose of the course," which is very general? No, that's what we're trying to avoid. The way we will look at objectives, we will see that the *entire training program*, from beginning to end, will revolve around the objectives. We saw earlier that the reason for training is that a person is doing something wrong, or not doing it well enough, or not able to do it at all. Put simply, *the objectives we prepare should be so specific that they tell in plain terms exactly what the person will be able to do at the end of the training.* This is not as easy as it may sound.

When we start our training, we may think we know exactly where we are going. *But do we really know where the employees will be when we are through?* We are going to teach them certain things. Suppose they don't learn them.

- Will we know it?
- Suppose they get only halfway there. Who's fault will it be?
- How do we know that the particular training we have in mind will get them where we think they should be when we are through training them?
- How will we measure to see how successful they are in getting where we want them to be, and how successful we are in getting them there?
- Will we hold them accountable for not getting where we want them to be, or will we accept the blame?

These are questions that can go unanswered if we do not have a good set of objectives, and the chances are pretty good that there won't be much success in our training.

We talked earlier about making a work analysis chart. One thing that this tells us is *where the employees are now*. It doesn't make much sense to start our training unless we know where the employees are when we start to teach them. If they are too far ahead of where we are starting, they will become bored and the training will be wasted. If they are too far behind where we start, we will leave them in the dark, and again the training will be useless. The analysis will tell us exactly where they are so far as job performance is concerned, although it won't tell us how far they will be able to go in what length of time. It will tell us what they are doing right and what they are doing wrong. The job analysis chart will tell us where we want them to be when the training is over. *The difference between the two is what they need to know.* We have to decide if we are going to try to fill the whole gap by training or if we are going to let the employees fill some of it on the job.

Figure 6.1 shows us how we determine what training is needed and helps us determine our objectives. Training is the

**Figure 6.1 Determining Training Requirements
and Training Objectives**

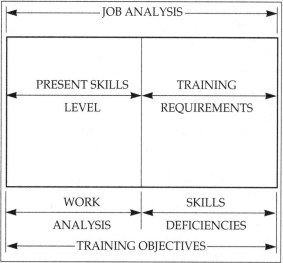

difference between the expectations (job analysis) and the present skills level. Since the objectives will tell us what the trainees will be able to do at the end of the training, they encompass both the present skills and the deficiencies, if we feel we can overcome all of these deficiencies in our training effort. The objectives have to be realistic, of course. The three main characteristics of any training objective are that they must be

1. measurable
2. observable
3. doable (accomplishable)

This means that when I make a commitment to employees that says they will be able to do something when the training is over, it should be something that we can measure and watch being done. It should also be a promise that can be kept. It shouldn't be something that we hope someday the employee will be able to do but only with a lot of practice. It should be something we can accomplish during the training.

Only when we get the items to be learned down so that we can specifically point to them one at a time (and step by step) are we able to prepare a training program that will accomplish our purpose of training. The objectives should be stated in this manner. Let's take some examples and see how objectives look. For instance, we have a group of salespeople who are making errors on their sales slips. After analyzing their work, we decide that even with some needed changes in the way the slip is made up, training is still necessary. Here are some examples of objectives for a training program for salespeople:

1. Teach the employees how to fill out sales slips.
2. Train them to stop making errors.
3. Make them understand sales slips.

The first one is probably the most common for most training programs: "Teach them how to . . . ." The first thing that is wrong with this objective is that it is written in terms of the teacher's action during the course rather than the employee's action at the end of the training. In other words, the main action is the *teaching*. *The main purpose of the training should be learning, so the objective should be stated in terms of what is to be learned.* The purpose of this learning is to enable the employee to be able to do something, so the objective should be expressed entirely in these terms. "But wait," somebody says. "This objective says the employees will be taught how to fill out the sales slip. What's wrong with that?"

The trouble is that this is not what we found the problem to be. We found the problem to be *too many errors*. The purpose of the course is to reduce the *errors*, so the objective should deal with the errors. It may be that they know how to "fill out sales slips." Maybe they don't. But how will we know when they are able to fill them out? Only when they start filling them out with fewer errors than they now have. How many fewer errors? The objective will have to tell us that also. This first objective does not deal with errors at all. But the next one does: "Train them to stop making errors."

Again we find that this one is written with the action centered around the trainer rather than the employees. It does deal with errors, though, so let's see if it will suit our purpose as an objective. At first it looks just like what we want—something that will eliminate errors. But are we going to eliminate *all* errors from all sales slips by everyone? If we think so, then we may have a sad surprise waiting for us at the end of the training session. It isn't very realistic to think that any kind of training is going to stop all errors. We are going to have to face reality in our training objective and decide how many errors we will be able to tolerate. This objective aims in the right way, but it still doesn't give us enough reality to guide us in our training.

The third objective is also one that is common but is by far the most useless of all: "Make them understand sales slips." The expression "make them" is not very encouraging to the employees. It sort of says to them, "You have been getting away with these errors long enough. Now we are going to *make you* see the light!" But we go from such a harsh term as "make you" to a term that can mean anything to anyone: *understand*. It's as though we are now apologizing for saying we were going to make them do something by watering it down to saying that we really aren't going to make you do anything in particular. What do we mean by *understand*? People seem to know exactly what the word means, but when you get down to it, you find that each has something different in mind. Let's listen in on a conversation between a training consultant and a supervisor eager to start training activity. It goes like this:

"You all ready to start training?"

"Yep. Just about. This is going to be a good session, too."

"Could I see your objective?"

"Well, I really don't have anything formal written out."

"You have it in your head?"

"I have in mind what I'm going to cover, but I didn't think I'd write out anything specific until I had the training completely organized."

"You mean you have just about organized the course but don't have an objective in mind?"

"Well, I know what I want to teach, if that's what you mean."

"But you don't know what you want the students to be able to do when you are through training them?"

"Sure I know!"

"What?"

"I want them to understand the framus machine."

"What do you mean, 'understand'?"

"I mean *understand*! They either understand it or they don't."

"How will you know when they understand it?"

"When they know all about the framus machine."

"*All* about it?"

"Yes, *all* about it. This is going to be an extensive course."

"Will they be able to build one in their basement?"

"Of course not!"

"Oh, then you don't want them to know *everything* about the framus machine?"

"No, I just want them to *understand* it." (Which is where we came in on this conversation!)

Let's look at the word "understand." Sometimes it's hard to realize the problem that arises with words like this that seem to have a specific meaning but in reality do not give us something we can measure, or even define. Suppose we have an office full of word processors. All of the employees are trained on how to use the processors, and use them well. A new employee comes into the office and the boss asks, "Do you understand how these things work?" What the boss is asking is, "Do you know how to type data, store it, transmit it by e-mail?" not how to repair or explain the inner workings of the processor.

Now with this same situation, suppose one of the people working on a processor begins to have trouble storing the data. The usual functions aren't getting the results. He asks, "Does anybody understand how this thing works?" Again, it's the same question, but an entirely different meaning. This time it's not how to use the processor to do routine work, when all functions are working. This time the person is trying to find out how to get it to do something it's supposed to do but isn't. In neither case does the question mean, "Can anyone explain the mechanism inside the processor?" Going a step further, imagine that the processor indeed is not working and has to be taken to the computer repair shop. When this model is brought in, someone asks, "Does anyone understand how this thing works?" Same question, different meaning for the word "understand." This time, the question is to find out if anyone is able to repair this particular model of processor.

So when we make our objectives, we need to steer clear of words like this that may give us a lot of trouble when we get to the end of the training and try to find out if the trainee has actually reached the objective we had stated—or promised!

So we see that the word "understand" is not a very good word to use when we are trying to express our objectives in precise terms. This means that the third objective fails on every count. But a good objective can be prepared for this training program. Let's look at some more and see how they hold up. We have found that the action should be on the part of the learner, so we'll start all of our objectives with: "The employee will be able to . . ."

1. Fill out sales slips without making so many errors.
2. Fill out sales slips with no more than one error.
3. Fill out sales slips with an average of 50 percent fewer errors a day.

Number 1 tells us what the goal is but unfortunately fails to give us an objective that is completely measurable. If employees made *one less error a year*, they would be meeting this objective. We just don't know how much improvement is expected. We probably could meet this goal by telling the employees something like, "These errors are costing the company $1.25 apiece to correct. From now on, this money will come out of your paycheck." No doubt the number of errors would be reduced considerably, but after a few paychecks came out with the deductions, the number of employees may be reduced also.

Number 2 tells us specifically how many errors will be tolerated but may be an objective that will be hard to reach. It is almost an impossible goal and does not allow for anyone to have a "bad day." It also does not specify the time limit on the one allowable error. "No more than one error a day, a year, a career"? When we give the objectives, they should be realistic enough that they can be reached by those being trained. Also, we should set objectives that are realistic from a training standpoint. *Remember, we are going to measure the effectiveness of our training by how well the objectives are met.* If the objective is impossible to meet and the employees can't do what we said they should be able to do, then we are admitting our training efforts weren't very good. In reality, the training may have been very good; it's just that the objectives were bad.

Number 3 gives us a better target to shoot at because it tells us what we are trying to improve by a *specific amount*, in a *specific time period*. It also tells us that this is to be done on an *average*

OBJECTIVE:

The employee will be able to fill out sales slips with a maximum of 2% errors in any given month... and no more than six errors in a day.

basis so that there will be room for a few bad days. But even though a time period is given, we don't know how the average is to be figured. What is the average based on? Two days? Two months? Two years? We don't know. The objective just isn't measurable the way it is written. But it has the basis for a good, realistic, measurable objective. For instance, we could add a few words and it would be more meaningful: "The employee will be able to fill out sales slips with an average of 50 percent fewer errors next month than were made this month." Now we know the time limits, and we have something to compare the new results with. We have a specific amount of improvement to measure. We can count the number of errors this month, then count the number made next month, and see if next month's is half of this month's. There is nothing mysterious about it now. We have set up an objective for our training. If the training is good enough, we will successfully meet our objective, and if it isn't, we won't meet the objective. We have stated the objective in terms of employee action. We have defined the object of the training (to reduce errors). We have said how much improvement we want and when we expect to get it. (We can leave out the word "average" since it has no real meaning to us now.)

We must be careful not to try to find a "mold" to pour our objectives into. Each objective should stand alone and aim at one

job and one training program. Depending on the needs of the job, the objective might appear quite different even in the same situation. For instance, let's assume we want to train a clerk to file letters and documents in an office. We have two choices in our approach. We can assist the clerk in learning all elements of the filing system, that is, the index system, the cross-reference procedures, the meanings of various headings, etc. Or we can take the clerk through typical documents to be filed to learn how these are handled. The first method would cover all conditions, but would take longer. The second approach would take less time but would not be as thorough. *The objectives would be quite different.* We might state them as follows:

1. When given all types of documents to file, the employee will be able to correctly place them in the file according to the established office procedure.
2. The employee will be able to file certain documents (specify types) correctly, that is, by the procedure now used in the office.

What makes the difference in these two objectives? One is expressed in terms of filing all the documents, the other in terms of only specific ones. Note that nothing is left to guesswork. When only certain ones are to be filed, they are specified. The word "correctly" is defined as "the procedure now used in the office." Presumably this procedure is written down somewhere so everyone will know exactly what is meant by this word. Note how much more specific all of this is than the kind of objectives we usually find at the beginning of courses: "The purpose of this course is to teach a better understanding of the office filing system." Or we might find: "In this Office Appreciation course, the clerks will learn about the office filing system."

Let's look at another example and see how important it is that we spell out the necessary restrictions as well as the conditions under which the work is to be done. A certain supervisor is in charge of several employees who repair small appliances of types A, B, and C. The supervisor trains new employees. Pause for a moment and see what you can write as an objective for such training.

Hopefully, you did not say, "The employees trained will understand how appliances A, B, and C work." What would be wrong with such an objective as this? What does it tell us? Will they have to be able to explain "how they work" to anyone? Will they have to be able to build one? Do they have to know how they work to repair them? Maybe the answer to all of these questions is "yes," but remember that none of the questions covers the real reason for the training. They were not being trained to explain anything to anybody. The training was not to teach them how anything works. They were not being trained to build anything. They were being given this training to make it possible for them to *repair* the appliances. If it takes knowing all of these things to be able to repair appliances, then they will have to learn them, but still the objective is to train employees to repair appliances.

How would this be as an objective for the supervisor? "When appliance A, B, or C comes in for repair, the employee will be able to identify and repair the trouble." Did you have something close to this? Maybe you went a little further and built in some more restrictions. There should be a few added. For instance, how long will the employee have to do the identifying and repairing? Most people could probably repair the appliances given enough time. But the customers can't wait that long. We might have added the phrase, "Repair the trouble in the time limits set on the repair-time expectancy chart," or ". . . within the maximum time limits set in our quotation guide." Without these restrictions, we will never know when we have reached our objective. (The employee, now 75 years old, keeps saying, "I can do it, I can do it," his voice trailing off into the shadows.)

Why did we add the word "identify"? Without it we would have the supervisor saying, "There is a short in the timer, Charlie. See if you can fix it." If the supervisor has to identify the problem, then half of the work may already be done. If we don't put it in, we have no right to expect Charlie to be able to identify the trouble. And worse yet, our training may *not* be geared only to train Charlie to find the source of trouble. What we may do instead is to set up our training by telling and showing Charlie what to do if he has this kind or that kind of trouble, without ever telling him how to find out what kind of trouble he has. When we include it in the objective, we see it there and do what is necessary to get Charlie to meet this objective. We have an easy task of measuring whether Charlie has met this objective:

We simply give him several small appliances of type A, B, or C that have come in for repair and see if he can identify and repair them in the time allowed. Since we will never be able to give him all the troubles that might appear, we can restrict the objective even more by listing the types of troubles he should be able to handle, such as shorts, open circuits, broken parts, etc. Or we might put it another way by saying, "The employees will be able to identify and repair at least 90 percent of the troubles that come in in a month's time," adding the time limitation for doing the repairing. Now we have another very easily tested objective. Count the problems that come in, determine the ones that Charlie can solve, figure the percentages, and the test is finished!

ACCOUNTABILITY—WHO?

One important point that is often overlooked in talking about objectives is *who is going to be accountable for a failure to meet the objectives*? Let's look at an example.

Charlie is seen operating a piece of machinery on the line in a dangerous way. The foreman stops him immediately and goes through a short training session with him. The session consists of the foreman going through the complete operation twice, slowly, with Charlie across the machine from him. The foreman finishes the second demonstration and asks, "Do you see now, Charlie?" "Yes, sir," is the reply. The foreman leaves, but a short time later is called back because Charlie has been hurt on the machine. The injury isn't serious, but the foreman is furious because an investigation shows the injury came about as a result of an incorrect use of the machine by Charlie.

Now who really was at fault here? If you think Charlie, you will have a lot of people agreeing with you. In the investigation, the foreman was cleared because he had spotted the incorrect operation by Charlie, stopped the operation, and did on-the-spot training. On paper this looks good, and the foreman and Charlie may think that the fault was really Charlie's. But let's look a little closer and see that the foreman got off a little too easily.

First of all we have to give the foreman a word of praise because he did so many things right in the beginning. Just being alert enough to spot the improper action by Charlie is commendable; stopping him immediately was excellent. (There was no reason to let Charlie run the risk of injuring himself.) His decision to do training right on the spot was certainly the thing to do. But because he hadn't learned the rules of setting objectives and then measuring them, his training all went for nothing.

In fact, *the training may have been a factor in causing the injury.* Both the foreman and Charlie probably ended the training session with confidence in Charlie's ability to do the job correctly. With this confidence Charlie went back to work and immediately proved that the confidence was misplaced. The truth is that the training was done poorly from many standpoints.

Later we will discuss some specific things about on-the-job training, so we will skip some of that discussion until then. For the time being, let's concentrate on the accountability for the failure to meet a satisfactory training objective, that is, Charlie doing the job in a correct manner so as to prevent his injury.

As we will see later, the foreman's technique of training was very poor. He failed to follow an accepted method by telling him, showing him, then getting *Charlie involved in the same process.* He also violated a prime rule by showing Charlie how to do the job while *facing* him, thus having everything in reverse for Charlie. But the most serious rule violated by the foreman was letting *Charlie* decide when he knew how the job was to be done, without even letting him demonstrate his newly acquired skill. ("Do you see now, Charlie?") There was no effort to let Charlie demonstrate that he had reached the sought-after objective. Charlie wasn't given a chance to go through the operation during the training session, under the watchful eye of the foreman. When he was asked if he understood, he probably thought he did. Even if he didn't, he was put on the spot by the foreman who had just gone through the step-by-step procedure *two* times. If he said he didn't understand, the foreman might have replied, "I don't see how you can be so dumb, Charlie! Here I've shown you twice how to do it and you still can't do it. I don't know what else to do."

No, we can't blame Charlie for this accident, regardless of what the investigation may have shown. *The important thing to remember is that supervisors must be accountable for the results of their people. The supervisors' training effort is the difference between good and bad, safe and unsafe, correct and incorrect operation.* We can only leave the employees to do their jobs when they have demonstrated that they have met the prepared objectives in such a way that they tell us exactly what we expect the end result to be. We can place the blame on the employees for their mistakes only when they have been through the steps we plan in our training, reach the objectives satisfactorily, demonstrate they can do what it is they were trained for, and *then commit an error.*

With due credit to the foreman, he no doubt felt Charlie hadn't listened or paid attention. We can hear him say, "But Charlie! Don't you remember? I *told* you to hold it this way." This was the foreman's undoing. He relieved himself of any responsibility simply because he *told* Charlie. Telling is not teaching.

Now let's look at this last example and relate it to what we have said about objectives. (You might want to read the case again.) What was the foreman's objective in the brief training session he had? "Well, I just wanted to teach him to do the job correctly and safely." But that doesn't fit our example of preparing objectives. Also, what about the measurement of his objectives? If his objective was to "teach" Charlie how to do the work satisfactorily, and to him "teaching" was telling and showing, then he met this much of the objective. He did go through some motions and probably a lot of talking. To the foreman, this was teaching. But the proper learning did not take place.

Stop here for a minute and try to write some realistic objectives for this little training session. (Remember that they must

take into consideration the conditions under which the work is to take place and the expected performance.)

Now try something else. Tell how you would *measure* to see if the objectives have been met.

What about this as an objective for Charlie's training: "Under normal working conditions Charlie will be able to operate his machine in accordance with the standard operating manual, following all the prescribed safety rules."

You may have worded it differently, but the basic facts to be included are that he is to be able to operate the machine correctly and safely, under normal working conditions. We may want to spell out more clearly what are "normal working conditions" if there are any peculiarities, or we may want to be more specific about "in accordance with the standard operating manual" if that doesn't give us enough information.

Now what about measuring this objective? It's not complicated. Just let Charlie start up his machine and watch him (after the training is over, which included his doing work on the machine).

CONCLUSION

We see that the foreman was incorrect in several of his efforts. That's why he was so much to blame in the accident. He accepted Charlie's word—without any visual evidence—that the job could not be done correctly. If he had taken just one more step, he could have learned so much more. Accountability becomes a very important factor. It is meaningless, though, without a good set of objectives. We see from this simple illustration how much these objectives help us in preparing *and* doing our training. Maybe Charlie would still have had his accident, but had the foreman followed the steps we talked about (and will talk more about later), the blame would have been on Charlie for carelessness. The foreman would have had visual proof that Charlie at least knew how to do the job, even if he didn't do it correctly at the time of the accident.

QUESTIONS FOR SMALL GROUP DISCUSSIONS

1. Discuss the statement found early in this chapter, "The way we will look at objectives, we will see that the *entire training*

program, from beginning to end, will revolve around the objectives." In what ways is this necessary?

2. What part do the employee work analysis and job analysis charts play in helping us set objectives?

3. What is wrong with an objective that says, "This training program will teach the employee to fill out sales slips"?

4. List as many interpretations as you can for the word "understand" in the phrase ". . . will be able to understand the zigzag unit on the sewing machine."

5. What do we mean by the terms "restrictions," "limitations," and "conditions" in preparing objectives?

6. Write an objective for a training program designed to be used for training people who bag the groceries at the checkout counter. (Remember the keys are speed, packing, courtesy, efficiency, and anything else you put in.)

7. Now do the same thing for the clerk who operates the cash register at this same checkout station. Make up your own keys. (Discuss how you would measure both objectives.)

8. Where maintenance and repair work is to be done, why is the word "identify" important?

9. Discuss *accountability* in the case of Charlie and the foreman, where Charlie got hurt immediately after a short training session.

10. What was wrong with the foreman *facing* Charlie when he was training him?

11. Prepare an objective for someone reading and studying this chapter.

chapter 7

PREPARING TO TRAIN

Imagine what we would think and say if one of our employees came up to a new machine and said to us, "I'm not familiar with this machine, and I don't know what I'm going to make, but here goes." We wouldn't be too proud of our people if they started doing something that important without knowing a little more about where they were going and how they intended to get there. But is that too different from our starting to train our people without making proper plans ahead of time, and without knowing exactly what we were going to do during the training?

When we *study* about training, we are likely to talk in broad, general terms, but when we are *doing* training, we are engaged in something very specific. We should bring all of these things together that seem to be general in nature so we can see that we are talking about something that is *real* and something that can be *done on the job*. That's why we have looked at so many different examples. You will need to keep on making the application to your *own specific job*, though, for this to mean anything. When we talk about "preparing to train" in this chapter, be sure to think of these things as they fit *your* training needs and not something that will fit somebody else's. When we talk about going into training without having made the proper preparation, check and see if you fit this description. (The reason for this little sermon is to remind you that we have said that the *accountability* for reaching the objectives belongs to the supervisor. This means that the accountability for *planning* and *preparing* also falls on the supervisor!)

So far we have seen that we must make a work analysis of employees' activities to find out what they are doing now. Once we have done this, we know two important things: We know how the job is *organized* now, in case we want to change it to make it more efficient, and we know how the employees are *performing*, in case training is indicated. In other words, we know *where* the employees are and *what* the job is. This will be a big help when we start to do our preparation work. If the employees are not at the right place, that is, they can't do what we want them to do, we train them to perform differently. If the job is not what we want it to be, that is, if it is not organized efficiently, then we take steps to change it, also.

THE SUPERVISOR WILL HAVE TROUBLE

When supervisors start to prepare their training programs, they may find that several things are working against them. We have already seen that the employees may resent the authority that the supervisors represent. We talked about ways to improve this kind of attitude. But there are other barriers. One of the things that may cause supervisors trouble is that *they know too much.* The *supervisors* probably know the jobs from many angles and may have many years of experience. They know the background of how a type of equipment came into being. They know how the equipment operates, how it is repaired, and maybe even how it is built. They have probably turned out many units on this one or one like it over the years. No doubt they have many interesting experiences they could share. All of this is excellent, *if it is used correctly.* But it can work against a supervisor very easily.

Starting Beyond the Employee's Knowledge

For example, *the most common thing the experienced supervisor does wrong is to start beyond the employee's knowledge level in describing an operation or the details of the job.* Supervisors forget that the employees don't have the supervisors' same experience and background information. They forget that employees may not know the terminology being used. The employees may not even recognize the words describing the parts and actions of the equipment, and certainly not the trade jargon that always creeps in. It isn't enough to say, "Now if there is anything you don't understand, just ask me." We've already talked about the dangers in this approach.

It is equally ineffective to ask, "Do you understand these terms?" and continue if the employee says, "Yes." If we are going to ask employees if they understand something, we'd better be ready to have them prove it by *showing us* some kind of action or *telling us* in their words just what something means to them. Some supervisors find it helpful to have a list of words and start out by having the employees tell what these words mean to them. If there are names of parts, then the employee can point them out to the supervisor. Any of these methods is good to get involvement and to find out where the employee is before we start the training. It doesn't take much time, and it is time well spent. It will save getting far into the training session only to have the employee ask, "What do you mean by that word? I never heard of that before."

Telling Too Much Unrelated to the Training

Along with talking over the employees' heads, we have a similar problem of just plain *talking too much.* We have had a lot of experience, and a lot of interesting things have happened to us, so we start to share them with the employees. No doubt our stories are very interesting to them (maybe even more so than the training we're doing), so the more they listen, the more we tell. Finally time runs out, and we have failed to get around to the training or have not put in the time needed to be successful. The stories have been good and interesting, but the employees will have to give an account of their performance on the job, not on their ability to recall our stories. For this reason the employees deserve to have all of the time that is allotted to training *spent on training*.

Omitting Necessary Details

Talking too *little* can be a problem, also. Just as we can start over the employees' heads by using words that are not familiar to them, we can fail to fill in the gap and start beyond where they are. We leave out the things they need to know, perhaps because we can't imagine that anyone doesn't know these very basic things. Here again the problem is one of being so familiar with what we're teaching that we're unable to put ourselves in the shoes of an employee who lacks the same foundation. We should use the same methods we used before to find out if the employee really knows what we are talking about and is ready to start at the same point we're starting from. Involving the employees by getting them to tell you and show you where they are will serve to interest them in the training that is about to take place. If they don't know the things you are starting with, this will help show them the need for training; if they do know them, this will show you that you need to revise your efforts. Hopefully, the end result will be *both you and the employees starting at the same place*.

USE YOUR KNOWLEDGE

As an experienced supervisor you have a lot of knowledge about the job and about the employees that needs to go into the preparation work. We have already talked about the importance of putting yourself in the employees' position to refresh your mind on what someone with their experience knows about the job. This means trying to imagine what you might have known at that stage of your career, providing you had had the same experience, the same amount of training, and the same amount of time to learn these things. (Try to avoid saying, "If I had had their opportunities, I would have been a lot further than they are.") We have to admit, of course, that it is impossible to completely put ourselves in another person's shoes. We can't put together in our mind the same likes and dislikes, the same attitudes, the same prejudices, and we can't put in our hands the same skills, the same experiences, and the same abilities. To a certain extent we can put some of our attitudes into an employee's mind, but we can't put our capabilities into the employee's hands. All we have to do is recognize these limitations and gear our actions to them. We do the best we can to understand how it is to be in the other person's shoes and go on from there. Fortunately, when we do the kind of analyzing we have talked about, we know a lot already and can leave less to chance.

If we really know our people as we should and have evaluated their work performance regularly, then we have a fairly good idea of their strengths and weaknesses and a general idea of their personalities. These things are important when we start to put the training together because we should know how fast the employees can learn. We need to know those things that come easy for them and those things that come hard. If they learn the manual part easily but find it hard to remember the steps or other features of the job, this information should be built into the training. More time should be allowed for the training on the information side of the job and less on the manual side. The reverse would be true if they learned the facts easier than the part requiring eye–hand coordination. We should not assume, because an employee is doing poorly now on one of these and well on the other, that this is an indication of a natural talent for learning. It may be that previous training and experience have given the employee more of one than the other.

It isn't too hard to find out where the individual's natural talents lie, but we should be careful not to make up all-inclusive categories (even as we have done in the paragraph above). A person may have a natural talent for learning certain types of information, such as long series of facts, sequences, numbers, etc., but be very poor at remembering *conceptual* ideas, where the facts must be put together in proper order to come up with a conclusion. Some people may have a talent for *forming* things with their hands almost as if they had "eyes in their fingers," but may not be able to react very well when they are required to use their eyes in *timing* certain events with their hands. Trying to coordinate their hands and eyes may be very hard for them. Other people may find the reverse to be true. They may be able to do a fine job of coordinating but have "rough" hands when it comes to doing any finish work that requires some sensitivity of touch.

Why do we have to worry about the individual's personality, likes and dislikes, prejudices and biases? Because we can make these things work for us if we try, and if we don't, then they may work against us. In Chapter 3 we talked about how certain words may spark resentment, hence keeping us from communicating very well. If we know the employee well enough, we will know that there are some things that have a tendency to evoke emotional responses. If this is the case, the training is too important to waste just because we got the employee upset over something that may have nothing to do with the actual training. Even if we don't know of such things, we need to be on the lookout and make a mental note if we see signs of emotions coming to the surface. This is why we need to try to avoid making fun of any groups of people or referring to classes of workers as "you blue-collar workers" or "the craft people" or "all the union hoods." This kind of humor or slang is too dangerous, and the risk of getting the person off the track in thinking is too great to bother with. (Of course, crude humor or filth never has its place, and it goes without saying that this kind of so-called humor can ruin the best of training programs.)

There will be training that we have to do where the employees are complete strangers to us. We will barely know their names and little else. We will know nothing of their capabilities or their personalities. They will be new to the job and bring virtually no experience with them. Their knowledge of the names and parts of the equipment and the terms we will use will be limited or nonexistent. If this is the case, then is all we have said going to be useless to us? We will have no chance to do a work analysis on them, so how will we know their weaknesses and strengths? We will not have a chance to observe where their natural talents lie and what things come hard to them. How are we going to deal with this problem? It is indeed very much of a problem, but not an impossible one to solve. There are many things that we can do to find out quickly what the employee can and can't do. Personnel records will help us. There are questions to ask and things to let the employee do that will give us a great deal of information before we start to train.

This is such a common and important problem to solve that we have reserved a special place for it in Chapter 9. There we will try to solve these problems with specific things the supervisor can do right on the job. For the time being, though, we will deal with those employees who have had some experience in some kind of work that is reasonably similar to what they are doing now. When we get to the specific steps in on-the-job training, we will see that the actual method does not depend upon these facts. We can use the *steps* without knowing these things. We need the background information to do the preparing for training and to decide how we will go about doing it, but the step-by-step method will serve us equally well with a brand new employee or an experienced one.

PREPARING AN OUTLINE

While much of our training on the job is informal, a certain amount of it is done at a specific time, measured, and recorded as having been done. For this type we need to prepare a little more than usual, especially if it is going to go on the employee's record. We would not want to be in the situation of not doing a good job of preparing for the training that some day might make the difference between the employee getting or not getting a promotion or raise. Since this is the case, we should prepare some kind of outline before going into the actual training. There is no set way to make this outline, but it should contain certain information that will help us before, during, and after the training.

What information would we want in a planning outline for training? We would want the important facts we learned from the work analysis we did on the employee; we would want the main points of the job analysis chart (probably the chart itself); we would want any notes that are important to understanding the strengths and weaknesses of the employee being trained; we should be sure the outline contains the objectives and how we plan to measure them; we would want any background information that might be helpful. However, *we should not think of this*

	TRAINING GUIDE
	Work Analysis
	(important facts)
○	▨▨▨▨▨▨▨
	▨▨▨▨▨
	Job Analysis
	(main facts)
	▨▨▨▨▨
	▨▨▨▨▨
	Employee Strengths
	and Weaknesses
○	▨▨▨▨▨▨▨▨
	Training Objectives
	▨▨▨▨▨▨
	▨▨▨▨▨
	Other Information
	▨▨▨▨▨
	▨▨▨▨▨▨
○	

as an official personnel file. This should not be considered as something very formal, but rather just notes to ourselves that will make the training go better for the employee. If we make this a part of the employee's permanent record, we should be sure that it is never used for *any other purpose* than as a guide for training. Things such as this have a way of getting misused at a later time by those who do not know the purpose of its existence.)

The purpose of this outline (or *guide* or *trainer's notes* or whatever we choose to call it) is to set the direction for our training and make it easier to instruct the employee in an efficient manner. It should include all of the necessary information as to what will be *said*, what will be *shown*, what the *supervisor will do*, what the *employee will do*, what kind of *time allotments* will be made, what kind of *aids* will be used in the training, and anything else that we think is good to have. One of the most important things to put in this outline is a note about the kind and frequency of *follow-up training* that will be done. As we will see later, much of what we do and say in the training session may be lost if there isn't some kind of follow-up training or check made to see that the training really "took" the first time.

TIMING IS IMPORTANT

Let's note a few things about timing, from the standpoint of both when we do the training and how long the training session lasts. There are many factors to be considered concerning the proper timing. There are times of the day that do not lend themselves to training, and there are times that are much better than others. The *length* of the training session will have a great deal to do with the amount of learning that takes place. There are problems with finding the necessary time to do the training and still take care of the other responsibilities of the job. There are training sessions that take more time than can be spared from the job at any one time. We have to decide how we will break up the training into meaningful parts and not lose the effectiveness of it. A decision has to be made, too, about how long a particular training session really will take (if we never have done this particular training before). Let's look at some cases and see how we might solve the time problem.

For instance, suppose we have a training program to give that experience has shown will take about four hours. We discover that we cannot take the employee off the production line for more than three hours at a time. There are then several possibilities to choose from:

1. Crowd all the training into the three hours.
2. Go until time runs out, then pick up at that point later.
3. Plan a two-hour session now and another one later.
4. Don't do the training until four hours are available.

Which of these is the best solution, or is there yet another possibility? Let's look at them one at a time and see what we can learn.

Number 1 is obviously wrong, but unfortunately it's the one we choose too many times. If we haven't got a good set of objectives and a plan to measure them, then we might try this and think we have been successful. ("After all, we got all the words in, didn't we?") Or we might argue that time isn't that critical and the four hours were probably arbitrary anyway, so why not rush things a bit and get everything in during the three hours. Another reason we give for crowding the training into a shorter time is found in the statement, "It takes so much time to get ready for training and to make the necessary arrangements to get the employee off the job that it doesn't make sense to go through it twice when we can get almost through in three hours." While we may not come right out and say these things, we may think them. It is a dangerous way to go so far as training is concerned, because it allows us to put training in the background as being something that has to be "gotten over with," and the sooner the better. We are back to saying that it really isn't important, so why worry whether it is good or bad? The only defense here is to say that we set some objectives that told us the employee would be able to do a certain thing at the end of the training session. If the training is done in a hurried manner, the objectives probably won't be met.

We must admit that time is always a factor, since *production* is what we are evaluating, not training. We probably will never find a perfect time. If the training is going to be too great a hindrance to the production schedule and we are going to have to reduce the time to three hours, then by all means we should be sure to *adjust the objectives accordingly*. Let's keep ourselves honest and admit that we won't be able to do the job we originally set about to do if the time for the training is cut by one-fourth. (If we *are* able to accomplish the objectives in less time, then we failed to do a very good job of planning in the first place.)

Number 2 suggests that we should go until time runs out, then come back later and pick up where we left off. Here again is something that we do a lot of times, not realizing that the place we stop may not be a very logical point to stop and start training. If we have done a good job of planning our training, we should be able to tell fairly well just where we will be at the end of three hours, but unless this is a good place to break off, we should look for a better solution. Another thing we know about this kind of stopping and starting of training is that if we haven't picked a very logical place to break, we may have caused a great deal of confusion. Also, we will certainly have to do quite a bit of reviewing when we start the second session so as to be sure and tie the two training efforts together. If we break off the training in the middle of a very important point, without finishing it, the employee may not only be confused, but may well have gotten the wrong idea altogether. Now that the job has been learned wrong, we have the problem of helping the

employee "unlearn" the error and then learning the correct procedure.

Number 3 suggests that we plan a two-hour session now and another one later. All right, this is as good a plan as any, but it should be noted that we still must look at the training objectives and see if they can be met in the time allowed. Do the two two-hour sessions satisfy our training needs? Can the employee meet our objectives at the end of the two sessions? Will breaking and training in two parts mean that we will have to actually allow more than two hours for the second session to get in a review of the first part? Do the information and skill we are trying to train the employee in lend themselves to two equal parts or is some other combination better (four one-hour sessions, some combination of one-and-a-half, two-, or several half-hour sessions)? We will see later that the training should actually be done in small "doses" of 15 to 30 minutes for each unit taught, so we should be able to come up with some kind of schedule that will give us satisfactory results. As we will see, the small bits of training are very effective, so finding the time is less of a problem than we might think. Not that we can't use the whole four hours if we have them, it's just that we will break this time into smaller sections when we actually do the training. (This means that our job analysis chart will come in handy because it is broken down this same way. It will be the thing that helps us the most in trying to decide whether to go the full three hours, then come back later for another hour, or come up with some other combination of hours.)

Choice number 4 ("Don't do the training until four hours are available") may help us prove a point about how important training is, and that we must have the proper time to suit our training needs, but while we are trying to win that war, we are losing the battle to improve the particular employee who needs the training. The employee continues to do the job incorrectly (perhaps even to the point of risking injury), produces less, or does poor-quality work (maybe even gets bad evaluations for it) while we try to prove our point. Holding out on the training to prove we are right may in reality be holding out on the employee who needs the training. The best way to win this battle is to show the set of objectives that has been prepared for the four-hour session, then rewrite them for the lesser time and show the difference the time makes in what the employee will be able to do. In the meantime, though, go ahead and do as much training as possible so that the job will be better than it is and the employee will know that you are interested. If more time is made available, then you will be in good shape to use it. If not, then you are on record as having asked for it and shown what

difference can be expected in the performance of the employee because the time is not available.

Now let's look at timing from the point of view of what is the best time of day to do the training. There is not much agreement on the *best* time of day to train, but there are some things to take into consideration. For instance, there are some built-in barriers to successful training that we can find fairly easily. If lunch is scheduled for noon, and we start what appears to be a lengthy training session at 11:45, the employee will have some problems staying with us as we near the 12 o'clock mark. Even if we tell the employee not to worry, we'll soon be through, that may not help. We may even decide to start at 11:45 and continue until 12:30, allowing the employee to take the full lunch hour at a later time. While this makes sense to us, it may not set too well with the employee, who may have plans to play ping-pong at lunch, or to go out with the other employees, or to do some shopping with a friend, or to meet someone at a certain time.

We will set a bad stage for the training under such circumstances, even if we try to find out if the employee has any plans: "You don't mind running over this a little bit, do you Gus? You can take your lunch hour when we get through." What can he say? Tell the truth, that he really has something else planned? Maybe so, and if he does, we should make it clear that it's all right for him to do what he has planned, and that the training will be scheduled again *very* soon. But not all employees feel free to tell the supervisor they have something else planned. They go through with the training, thinking all the time about what they could have done if they hadn't been tied up with training. Or they may spend the time wishing they had told the boss they really did have something to do. They may keep asking themselves, "Why didn't I ask him why the training had to interfere with *my* plans. Why couldn't he do a better job of making his plans?" Maybe we'll have a hard time finding good answers to Gus's questions!

The same thing goes for starting training that is likely to run into break or quitting time. Even if we have every intention of stopping in time, there is still that uncertainty about it, and the employee may be wondering if we *really* will stop. It just doesn't make sense to run the risk of spoiling good training by picking a time that may interfere with the success of the effort. This is especially so if some other time can be made available just as easily. Picking a time that may run into the employee's scheduled rest or quitting time gives the employee the idea that the training is secondary to the production job and shouldn't interfere with this any more than necessary.

So far as the other times of the day go, it must depend upon the local situation as to whether to have the training early in the morning or late in the afternoon. Sometimes the work schedule has to set the time for training, but this shouldn't be much of a problem if we do the training correctly. *If we get the employee involved and create enough interest, there just isn't a bad time to train.* If we follow the step-by-step methods discussed later in the book, we will have the employee very much engrossed in the activity. Since we will be giving the training in small bits, the employee isn't likely to get bored or tired, even if the training is done at the end of the day, although late in the workday is potentially the worst time to train.

WHERE DO WE TRAIN?

As we have already discussed, the training may be done at the job site, or it may be the "vestibule" type, where it is done close by to give the same atmosphere and use as much of the same equipment as possible. The choice will have to depend on many things. Will the training interfere with the other activities going on at the job location? Will there be enough room? Is there spare equipment available? Are there distractions that make good training difficult to accomplish? Will the other employees get in the way or cause a problem by looking on or making comments? These are some of the considerations that must be looked at when the place for the training is being selected.

The place is important and where possible should look the same as the work location. Since we are trying to teach how to do something better or how to do something new, we want the employee to do it on the job. If the trainee has to make too much of a change from the training to the real job, some of what has been learned may be lost. On the other hand, if the employee is trained under actual working conditions, less of what we have taught will be forgotten. Ideally, the training should be done at the work location, on the same equipment the employee will be regularly working with, *while the regular job is going on*. This way everything that is done in the training fits right into the normal, everyday work routine. There is no need for the supervisor to keep saying, "Now remember, when you get on the job, it will be slightly different from the way you learned it here." Sometimes this can't be helped, of course, and when we do have to go somewhere else, we should be sure to follow up back on the job to see that the employee has been able to make the adjustment.

If the training is to be done on the job, we should check in advance to see what problems might arise during the training session. We should see just what kinds of things will be going on *at the specific time* we will be doing the training. If we notice that at some particular time there is less likely to be interference than at some other time, we may even want to change the time we have scheduled. On the other hand, if we see that there is a particularly interesting problem that arises at certain times during the day, we may want to plan our training to take advantage of this.

The one thing we should be sure to do is to familiarize ourselves with all the things that may go on at the training location. If we can eliminate anything that might interfere, then we should arrange to take care of that. If there is some reason why we will need *special equipment* that might be tied up somewhere else unless we have reserved it, then that should be taken care of. Reservations should be made in advance, stating the day and the time of day we will need the equipment. It is both embarrassing and poor planning to start the training and suddenly discover that the key equipment is going to be tied up, and we will either have to do without it or reschedule the training. Any props or models that are needed should be on hand, checked out to be certain they work, and reserved for our training session. If we do these things, we may still run into some problems, but chances are that things will go a lot smoother as a result of the effort we have made to prepare for successful training.

CONCLUSION

So far we have seen that we must find out what the employees are doing *now* by making a work analysis of their activities.

Once we've done this, we will know two important things: We will know how the job is organized now—in case we want to change it to make it more efficient or effective—and we will know how the employees are performing. This will be a big help when we start to do our preparation work for training.

While much of our training on the job is informal, certain amounts of it are done at a specific time, measured and recorded as having been done. For this type we should prepare a little more than usual. We would not want to be in the position of not doing a good job of preparing for the training that some day might make the difference between an employee getting or not getting a promotion or increase in salary. Because of this, we should prepare some kind of outline before going into the actual training. We should get the important facts from the work analysis and the main points of the job analysis chart. The purpose of this outline is to set the direction for our training and to make it easier to instruct the employee in an efficient manner.

Timing is a very important factor to consider in our training plans. There are times of the day that do not lend themselves to training. The length of the training session will have a great deal to do with the amount of learning that takes place. The actual place where the training is done is important, and it should look as much as possible like the workplace.

If we consider all these things, there still may be problems, but the chances are that things will go a lot more smoothly as a result of the effort we have made to prepare for successful training.

QUESTIONS FOR SMALL GROUP DISCUSSIONS

1. Discuss the statement made in this chapter about barriers, "One of the things that may cause supervisors trouble is that *they* may be so familiar with a job that they can't relate."

2. A supervisor was training an employee to operate a small hand tool that had just come on the market. The tool was similar to the one the employee had been using but had some attachments that were not included on the one presently in use. The names of the attachments were different because they described the job that they did. At one point the supervi-

sor was heard to say, "By the way, I've been talking about these things assuming you understand what I'm saying. If you have any questions, be sure to let me know." What's wrong with these statements?

3. Discuss some of the problems that arise from the supervisor either talking too much or not talking enough during the training effort.

4. How can the knowledge of the employee's strengths and weaknesses in the job be helpful to the person preparing the training?

5. What consideration should be given to *timing* in our training efforts?

6. Discuss what problems might arise in *your* work situation if you had a need to train each of your employees for an hour at a time, and had to get this done in the next few days.

7. If you were to do the training mentioned in Question 6, what time of day would you choose? What reactions would you get if the training ran into a portion of their lunch or break time, or slightly past quitting time?

8. Suppose a change has just come out on how to fill out a time sheet or work report. You must discuss this *individually* with each of your employees. It will take about 30 minutes to go over the new method. Discuss where you would do this training and what arrangements you would have to make ahead of time.

chapter 8

HOW TO DO ON-THE-JOB TRAINING

So far we have been discussing the things necessary to prepare for on-the-job training. Now we will look at the actual processes to go through when the training begins. The methods discussed here—or variations of them—have been in use for many years. They have proven themselves to be practical and effective. Once the simple procedures described here are learned, they can be used in any kind of instruction where there is something to be done on a step-by-step basis. These methods have the advantage that they fit right into our remarks on setting objectives and measuring the outcome. All that we have said until now leads us naturally into a system whereby the employee takes an active part in the training. For the kind of results we want, there can be little room for a "passive" training program where the employee sits back and listens to the instructor do all the talking, all the demonstrating, all the explaining.

SELF-PREPARATION REQUIRED

In the last chapter we talked about the preparation that is required before the actual training is undertaken. The one thing we did not mention was the groundwork that supervisors must do to prepare *themselves* for the instructing they are about to do. If they do training fairly regularly, they won't have to do nearly as much preparing as they will if their training efforts are few and far between. But regardless of how frequently the instructing is done, there are certain areas in which supervisors should do review and self-preparation.

Obviously, the instructor should be familiar with the information contained in the manuals or specifications for the training that is to be done. The supervisor should review the source material thoroughly not only as a refresher on the way to do the job but also to check for any revisions that may have come along since last reading the manuals. (Hopefully there won't be many cases where the supervisor does not know the latest techniques, but there will always be the likelihood that some of the small details may have been changed or brought up-to-date.) Perhaps nothing can kill the effectiveness of training quicker than for the person doing the instructing not to know the material being taught. It is always embarrassing for the supervisor to be cor-

NEXT ORDER OF BUSINESS

rected by the employees for teaching the wrong data or for information that is out-of-date. Of course, if the supervisor *is* incorrect, then it is better if the employees point out the error during the training than for them not to find it out until later (or not at all). Certainly the supervisor should welcome any corrections the employees have. It would not be very constructive for the supervisor to be offended or show disgust at being corrected, since the whole purpose of the training is to be sure the employees have the right information and can use it correctly.

We have already talked about the importance of knowing the capabilities of the employees being trained. As we start our training, we would always do well to go back and take a look at their personnel records and see if there are any clues that will give us an insight into difficulties or problems we might expect to find. Here again is a chance to refresh ourselves as to the training the employees have had, how well they responded to this training, and any performance records that are available. Much of this may already be in our guide or outline that we have prepared for the training we are about to do, but anything that will give us even a little more background on the employee may make considerable difference in the results of our instructing. If previous efforts at training haven't been very successful, we may want to try a little different approach. If what has been done worked well, then we would want to start with that. This will help us avoid the mistake of saying, "I think I will try something different this time," not realizing that the last effort had extremely good results, and we are about to change that.

We will want to review our notes on how to communicate ideas and skills to employees effectively. We should look at books like this and see what the barriers to communication are and what things aid the transfer of information. As we have seen, often small things that seem insignificant may reduce the amount of learning by large amounts. A word, a phrase, a poorly chosen joke can all interfere with the learning process. But these are things that can be avoided, and it is just a matter of knowing about them and learning to be careful in what we say and how we say it. We need to think back and recall conversations we have had with the employees. How successful were we in getting our point across? Did we leave with the feeling that maybe they understood and maybe they didn't? Do we remember specific instances where something we said was *misunderstood*? Do we recall times when certain illustrations went a long way toward helping a particular employee see a point? Is there something about this person's background that makes one illustration much better than some other? These are the kinds of things we should look for and make notes about to use when the training actually starts.

Finally, we need to review the actual steps we will use in doing the on-the-job training. All that we have done so far has led up to this point, so we should make sure to refresh our memories on the best means of doing the actual instructing job. Several times we have pointed out that good teaching is not done accidentally. The ability to train others to do something is a skill that can be learned. It can be done poorly or well. It may come naturally to a few people, but *not to very many*. On the other hand, there are possibly some that may never be able to communicate well with others, but here again the number is very small. Of those who can't do a very good job of instructing others, there are very few who lack any ability to do so. The rest either don't know how, or don't use the knowledge they have, or *think* they are good at it and don't realize their shortcomings. But, like any skill, good instructing can be learned. Also, like any skill, one has to work at it to be good. For this reason, we should be sure to review the techniques discussed later in this chapter and be certain our plans include the use of these methods.

PREPARING THE EMPLOYEE

Once we have properly prepared ourselves for the training and have the necessary notes and information to help us do the best job possible, we can begin our training effort. The place has been chosen and inspected, the time has been considered and allotted, the employee has at least been alerted that training is to take place, so everything is ready. What is the first thing we do?

We begin by preparing the employees for the training. It would be simple enough just to go ahead and start the training, but remember, the employees haven't done as much preparing as we have. The employees certainly aren't in the proper frame of mind at this stage to receive the training, even though they know that we intend to begin now. Rather than jump into the training session, we must *first put them at ease*. Consider the following examples as opening remarks to make when you show up for the training:

1. "Hello, Sue. You ready to get this training over with?"
2. "Hiya, Sue. How are the kids?"
3. "Hi, Sue. I see you're still fouling up on the machine."

Which of these would be the best to open with? Number 1 may have been said in fun, but it may have set the wrong tone for the training. "If this is the way the trainer feels, then it must not be very important," Sue may say to herself. We certainly don't want to spend half the day in idle conversation, but neither do we want to jump right into the training. There is nothing wrong with using humor to put the employee at ease, but we should be sure the employee doesn't misunderstand what we're trying to do. Unfortunately, we can't come out and say, "Sue, I'm supposed to put you at ease, so relax, will you?" What we say must be sincere, but it must accomplish the objective of letting the employee know that what is coming up isn't going to be too painful. The question "Are you ready?" won't accomplish much since Sue isn't likely to say, "Well, not really. Why don't you come back some other day?" It's up to you to decide when she's ready, and if she isn't, then you should do whatever you can to get her ready.

Number 2 is a sincere question and one that is calculated to put the employee at ease. It doesn't have to be children, of course. It may be the husband, the new car, the vacation, a new recipe, a hobby, or anything that will remove some of the strain and nervousness of the situation. If the office is normally in a relaxed atmosphere, there will be less need to work at putting the employee at ease. On the other hand, if an unusually formal or distant attitude prevails in the office, the "putting at ease" stage is very important and necessary. Remember what we said—it doesn't have to take half the day, maybe just a couple of minutes—but the time is well spent if it relaxes the employee and she learns better, remembers longer, and makes the application quicker. This is just a brief "passing the time of day" thing, and may go like this:

"Good morning, Sue."

"Good morning."

"By the way, I notice people call you Suzie most of the time. Which is it, Sue or Suzie?"

"Most people call me Suzie."

"Which do you prefer?"

"Suzie, I suppose, although my husband calls me Sue."

"Husbands are that way! How is he?"

"Chuck's fine. Went fishing over the weekend and caught some fish, so he's feeling great today."

"Hey, that's good. Wish I could have a little luck with my fishing. Find out his secret, will you?"

"I'll try. I suspect it's luck, though, more than any secrets!"

"Maybe so . . . maybe so. Now, Suzie, about this training . . . ."

All of this took less than a minute, but look at the information we have, in addition to putting Sue at ease. We know her husband's name is Chuck. He likes to fish. She prefers to be called Suzie, but doesn't have any real feeling for one over the other. The next time we have some training to do with Sue, we will have some things to open the conversation with, providing we make a few

short notes for the record. Even while we do the training, we can refer to Chuck's luck at fishing if we need to make a point or keep her at ease. These things may seem unimportant, but successful supervisors learn to use these kinds of tricks to their advantage over and over again.

Number 3 probably doesn't need any comments, but the remark about "fouling up on the machine" is a good example of the poor attempt at humor we discussed earlier. About the only thing that could make this worse is to make these remarks in front of all the other employees. This would not only finish us off with Sue, but would probably ruin future efforts with the other workers also. Maybe we could get away with saying something like this to Sue, but maybe we just think we get away with it, when in reality Sue and the others resent what we say. If Sue actually is "fouling" up, she will know it and be offended by such an opening remark. The risk is too great and there is so little to gain; we just can't afford to start a training effort with a statement like this.

GUARANTEED LEARNING

There is another part to putting the employee at ease that is equally important to what we have already said. When we get into a discussion about the actual training, we should *guarantee the employee that the learning will take place*. Nothing will put the employee more at ease than this assurance. But can we really guarantee that the proper learning will take place? We can if we have done a good job of breaking down the work into small, realistic bits; and if we have made a good lesson plan to go with the good objectives we set; and if we properly prepare the employee for the teaching session; and if we go about our training in the correct way.

That's a lot of "ifs," but not an impossible task. We should believe in our own ability, or the employee certainly isn't likely to. The success comes from studying and practicing the things contained in this book. So what do we say when we discuss the training with the person to be trained? Here are three examples for us to look at. Which one comes the nearest to filling our needs?

1. "I know you can learn this, Dave, because I have taught it to a lot of fellows who were dumber than you."
2. "I'm not the best teacher in the world, Dave, but if you try hard, you should learn it all right."
3. "Don't worry about it, Dave; the way we'll go through this training, you won't have any trouble at all."

Of course, you really wouldn't say number 1, but maybe we say the same thing, just in different words. It's fine to give him confidence in your ability as a trainer, but not by suggesting that he is a little stupid. We want him to know that when people are put on this job, we think they have the ability to learn whatever is necessary to do the work. We could better prove the point by letting him know we have trained other men *just like him* and they learned without any trouble. What we need to do, though, is to get the employee's mind off himself and on the training. Assure the employee that the *training* is such that *it* guarantees success, rather than the teacher.

Number 2 is the apologetic approach that instructors often use to cover any shortcomings that may show up. Remember, we are trying to *put the employee at ease*, not show him how humble we are. When Dave's career is at stake, he may not appreciate this humility very much. Listen to how it comes out when Dave decodes what we have said, "I'm not a very good teacher, Dave, so it's up to you. If you get it, you'll get it on your own." That's not likely to go very far toward making Dave feel at ease. Notice how nicely we have shifted all the blame to Dave and removed any responsibility for results from ourselves: "If you try hard . . . ." Dave may wonder why we didn't try a little harder ourselves to learn to be a better instructor.

Number 3, of course, comes the closest to meeting our aim of shifting the emphasis from the employee to the training. It puts the responsibility for the learning on the manner in which *we* go through the training. It says that together we will share the responsibility for the learning, and together we will go through the training without any trouble. There is no indication that *only he* has the key to success. There is no idea that you have any doubt but that the training will work. It says that you must know what you are doing. All of these things will produce confidence and go a long way toward putting the employee at ease.

BUILDING INTEREST

Part of putting employees at ease must include interesting them in the training that we are about to do. We not only want to relieve their mind about their ability to learn the new procedure, but we want them to enter this training session with enthusiasm. There are a number of ways of doing this. We have already shown that there is little hope of developing enthusiasm in employees when it is absent in the instructor. The instructor must be sincerely interested in seeing that the employees learn all that can be learned about the job, and the instructor must be sure that this sincerity shows! The employee cannot develop interest in the job training if we merely pass the time of day, or talk about fishing and ask about the kids. The conversation must be brought around to a discussion of the job itself. Since there is no secret that the purpose of this session is training, there is no advantage in spending too much time in trivial talking. A certain amount is necessary and very important, but there is a limit to how long it can be helpful. After that it may start to interfere with the real reason for the supervisor being there.

"Say, Al, what do you think of this new machine? It sure beats the other one, don't you think?" This is a leading question, but *now* is the time for a leading question. At this point we want to avoid getting into an argument over the relative merits of the two machines, so we start out with a question, then answer it with a pretty positive opinion. Unless Al has some rather strong feelings about the new machine, he will probably go along with at least, "Yeah, it looks like it will do a good job." In case he does have a strong dislike for the new equipment, this will be a good time to find out about it. It's better to find out now than to discover it later when we have spent considerable time on training that may not be very effective.

We could lead the conversation more if we wanted to with, "I think you'll be surprised how much easier this equipment works than what we've been using, once we finish this training session." Here again we have put in a strong opinion, but that's the way we feel, and we want him to know it. We've even gone further and promised a "surprise" for him. This is part of the effort to build in some enthusiasm. But here again we have made it clear that we have no doubt that the employee *can and will* learn the things we are about to show him. Of course, these should not get to be "canned" statements that we use every time we start to do training. The thoughts expressed should be casual, sincere, and certainly not "sermons." When we use a leading statement it shouldn't come out as, "You're going to like this machine better than the old one because I say so. You're going to like this training and you're going to learn in spite of yourself!" While we wouldn't say just these words, what we do say shouldn't be interpreted that way, either.

SHOWING THE PERSONAL ADVANTAGE

There is one more step we should take before we start to do any training. We have put the employee at ease, have built some interest in the learning process, and know where we are going to stand when we train. It would seem that there is nothing left for us to do but begin the training. But there is one thing that will go a long way toward increasing the chances of success: We should try to convince the employee that there is some *personal gain* in the training. We have already talked about the "reward" and "punishment" approaches to getting people to learn. If we can do it, here is a good place to put in one of these. We wouldn't put it like this, but the two approaches would look like these:

1. "If you don't learn, you may be out of a job."
2. "If you learn this, you'll be on your way to a promotion."

The first one is of course too blunt, and we probably won't fire anyone for not learning just one thing, although it may come to this if the employee continues to fail to learn. Number 1 is the ultimate in punishment as a means of getting the employee to learn. It rarely serves to any advantage, but it is always good to have some kind of understanding as to the results if the employee isn't able to make it on the job. It's a good idea to have this understanding *before* the time comes to use the punishment, rather than spring it on people at the time you are ready to fire them or demote them. There are occasions when the employees are given some kind of demotion or at least not promoted if they fail to meet certain standards in the training program. If so, then these standards should be clearly understood and spelled out ahead of time so that there will be no misunderstanding at the end of the training period. It isn't likely that the best time to point these things out to the employees is at the time the training is to begin. Remember we have gone to great lengths to make the person feel at ease. All of this will be cancelled if we now tell them—just before we start the training—"Oh, by the way, you realize that if you don't do well on this training you will lose your job!"

The second approach—reward—is closer to what we would most likely use in trying to get them to see the personal gain from doing well on the program. We see one fault in promising a promotion—there may not be a promotion available to give. Or there may be several employees who are getting the same training and only the one who does the best will receive the advancement. It may well be that no one will be promoted as a result of taking this training. The idea that every training program that is successfully completed will end in promotion is false and will get us into more difficulty than we care to have. The idea, of course, is that the advancements come to those who know their jobs and do them well. The advancement may not come as a direct result of the training nor at the end of the training, but the training is one of the things that will give the

employee more knowledge of the job, and more skill in doing it. If we take this approach, then we can use the reward approach any time, but not to such a degree that it becomes meaningless. If it starts to sound like preaching, then the employee will tune us out and begin to get bored. We have to find a fresh and believable way to say, "Do well and you will be rewarded." (But this isn't too hard to do since basically we all believe this.)

Promotion and more money aren't the only rewards that motivate an employee to do well on the training. There are many, and you can make a list yourself, which might include:

- More self-satisfaction
- Easier work
- Less repetition
- More respect from fellow employees
- More responsibility because of added ability

From this list and the one you make yourself, you can find enough ideas to show the employees that they have plenty to gain by doing a good job of learning the material at hand and much to lose by not learning it. Just be sure not to limit the rewards to money and promotion alone, because there are many things that will be more lasting and offer more satisfaction in the long run.

AVOID TEACHING IN REVERSE

One thing that must be remembered in training people is to avoid showing them anything while we are *facing* them. We must always be standing or sitting *beside* them so that they will see the parts, the handles, the buttons, the equipment, everything from the same angle they will be working on them. When we face people, everything they see is reversed. Our left hand is on their right, the front to us is the back to them, etc. This means that when we walk up to their workbench or desk, we should be careful not to lean over and try to show them the operation, which is perhaps the natural way for us to do it. When we are showing the employees the steps to follow, and then when they are showing us how it is to be done, we want them to be not only beside us but as close as possible to the exact spot where they will be doing the work when we leave. The point here is that often we make the mistake of having the employees stand beside us and watch while we sit at their seat and operate the machine. Then we have them show us but allow them to continue to stand as we sit. *But this isn't where they will be working*, so we haven't got a real test as to whether they can do the job or not when they are seated.

Another way that we mislead employees in training is to stand beside them and show them while they are sitting down. While we demonstrate, we are standing, perhaps even gaining an advantage of movement by not having to sit down. They watch what looks like the correct way to do the operation only to find that they can't do it exactly as we did when they try it. We may even think the fault is theirs, when really we would have the same difficulty if we had to sit as they are doing. We just need to be sure that everything we do is done from the same angle, the same position, and that it looks the same to them as it will when they do it after we leave.

HOW TO DO ON-THE-JOB TRAINING

The things we have discussed aren't really as complicated and as formal as they may have seemed. If we take a close look at them, we will see that most of them are just a matter of using common sense. They usually take longer to tell about than to do. Now let's look at the simple, threefold process of actually doing the training. Basically, the steps are

1. Demonstrate the process (showing and telling).
2. Have the employee tell you (while *you* do it).
3. Have the employee do it (showing and telling you).

We will expand on these steps a little later, but first let's see what we have said. In the same position the employee will be in when working, with the employee beside or slightly behind us, we go through the operation, telling the employee at the same time what we are doing. Then we go through the operation again, this time having the employee tell us what we should do before we do it. The final step is to allow the employee to go through the operation, but tell us each step *before* doing it. (As we will see, this last step is very critical from a *safety* stand-point.)

What would be wrong with saying, "Okay, Buck, take the lever here and go through the steps as I explain them to you," as the first step in the training session? This would be a good way to get Buck involved, but he would be involved in the wrong way. One of the important things we must remember is that we must *protect the employees* around dangerous equipment. If there is a possibility that they might get hurt, and we start out by letting them operate the machine without showing them the safe way, then we may be setting them up to harming themselves. The rule is simple: *Never begin a training session by letting the employees do it themselves, even if we are telling them step by step what to do.* (Some may argue letting the employees go through the operation once allows us to see their weak points. The trouble is, though, that their "weak points" may be in cutting off their fingers!)

Note that while the process is simple enough, the employees get considerable practice under very close supervision and yet are still able to think for themselves in the operation. What we provide is guidance not only to see that they do the work correctly, but safely. The first step, the *guidance* step, is the only one where the instructor is performing all the "talking" and "doing." The second step indicates if there was any misunderstanding on the part of the employee, but protects the employee by letting the instructor still do the operation. The third step has the employee performing both the telling and the showing but still provides protection by having the employee explain each piece of the operation *before* doing it.

Let's see how it works. We want to teach a clerk a single operation of filling out a particular ledger sheet. After all the preliminary activities of preparing the employee for the training have been taken care of, we begin like this:

- Step 1. We take the ledger and point by point we go through and fill it out, explaining each item as we go. When we have finished, we should have a completed ledger sheet and a completed explanation.
- Step 2. We will still have the pencil, but the clerk tells us what goes in each space, column, and row. We do not write any-

thing until it is the right information. We correct the employee as necessary but only put down the information that is supposed to be on the sheet.

- Step 3. Now the employee has the pencil and begins to fill in the ledger sheet. *But* the clerk does not write anything before telling us what it is going to be and also *until we agree* that it is the right information.

In this example there was no need for us to "protect" the employee because the operation was not dangerous. But we have done two things that will help us later. First, we have kept the employee from doing anything wrong or seeing anything wrong on the sheet and have kept the employee from developing any bad habits. Next, we have developed a habit ourselves of preventing the employee from doing anything in the training without telling us first. If we get into a dangerous situation, this habit will help prevent serious accidents. Now let's look at another example, this time showing Chuck how to operate a small hand tool.

- Step 1. Standing beside Chuck, facing the workbench just as Chuck will be doing when he is actually doing the job, we go through the operation. We explain the operation before we do it so Chuck will know what to look for; then we perform the operation so he can see that we actually did it that way. "You see, Chuck, the starter hole has been made with the punch by the person up the line who operates the die press. With the drill running, you place the bit directly over the starter hole. (The instructor places the drill thusly.) Now without applying any pressure, you set the bit into the starter hole. (Place the bit as directed.) The weight of the drill will start the bit into the metal, so let it rest on the starter hole until you can see small bits of shaving begin to appear. (Let the weight of the drill start the boring operation until these shavings begin to curl up around the bit.) Now you will have to apply just enough pressure to keep these shavings coming out at an even pace. If they slow down, slightly increase the pressure, and if they come out too fast, let up slightly. Continue until the hole is through. (Proceed with the boring until the bit goes through the material.) With the drill still running, bring it out slowly. (Pull it out of the hole.) When the bit is clear, turn the drill off and replace it in the rack. (Do so.)"

Note that the instruction is done in small bits, matching the job analysis chart we have earlier made for this operation. We are going to expand on Step 1 a little later to show how more practice and instruction can be added, but for now note that we have tried to keep each bit of instruction small by doing only one thing at a time. Each time, the statement is made first as to what is to be done, then that part of the operation is performed. The small steps are logical and complete in themselves. There is only one thing to remember at a time since no two operations are linked together or are dependent on each other. Now we go to Step 2 and see that we again use these same small bit-by-bit pieces to show how the whole job is accomplished.

- Step 2. A new piece of metal is brought out and the drill is held *by the instructor*. "Okay, Chuck, what is the first thing we do?" From now on, the operation looks just like the last one, except Chuck is telling the instructor what to do, rather than the instructor telling Chuck what he is about to do. Again, *the telling comes first*, then the doing. If Chuck gets the operation wrong or out of sequence, the instructor does what is necessary to correct him. It may be a pause that indicates that Chuck has come up with the wrong thing. It may be a few words that will lead Chuck to remember the step that is required. ("What do we watch to see if the hole is being bored evenly?")

If Chuck has completely missed the steps and shows that he does not have any of the operations right, it may be best at this stage to go back to Step 1 and start over. The instructor again does the telling and the showing, breaking the steps down to even smaller bits if possible. The good part of this is that the job analysis chart allows us to keep breaking the training into smaller and smaller bits until we have one small enough to suit the employee and the training situation. If necessary, the placing of the bit into the starter hole can be a complete training program in itself!

When you are satisfied that Chuck has been able to tell you each step of the way, he takes the drill and begins the operation. Remember, though, that he has only been *telling* you, and *watching* you, and not applying any manual skills. If touch will help him get the idea of the right amount of pressure then it may be well to repeat Step 2, with the employee placing his hand on yours while you go through the "pressure" steps. This will make Step 3 easier because he now has the "feel" of the drill going into the metal and knows about how much pressure is required to complete the boring. Allowing him to place his hand on yours during the second step will also let him get the feel of pressure being released when the bit comes through the metal on the other side. If there is a danger of going too far when the bit finishes the boring, it will be important for Chuck to "feel" the drill in operation in your hand before he tries it.

- Step 3. This step is just like the others in that it is still a telling and showing procedure, but this time Chuck is doing the whole thing by himself. He takes the drill, starts the hole, uses the right amount of pressure, finishes the hole, withdraws the bit, turns off the drill, and replaces it on the rack. *But before anything is done, he tells you what he is going to do, and you agree before he actually does it.* If he is about to do something wrong, you stop him immediately. You correct him, trying to get him to tell you the proper procedure, and when he does, allowing him to go ahead and perform the operation. Here again, if it becomes obvious that he is not ready to perform the task, then you can go back to Step 2 or Step 1. If it is a skills problem, then go back to Step 2. If it is a procedural problem, go back to Step 1. (In other words, if he can tell you what to do, but can't do it, he needs to see you go through the operation again, perhaps with his hand on yours. Since he knows *what* to do, there is no need to go back and start Step 1 again. If he can't tell you the procedures in the right order, go back and start again, this time with smaller bits of training than before.)

TELL THEM HOW

So far, we have gone through these steps just by telling the employees what we were going to do, but not *how*. If the operation is such that it is complicated and needs the steps explained in more detail, it is good to add one more item to each step. We not only tell them what we are going to do, but before we do it we tell them how we will do it. In the case of the clerk, it may have been that there was no reason to explain how we were going to perform the task. If we said we were going to put "25" in a certain space, it was obvious that we did it by writing it in with a pencil. On the other hand, if we got the figure by adding two figures, then we would want to be sure to show this as the way to do it. "We get the 25 by adding the 12 and the 13 from these two rows." When we were training Chuck, it was easier to tell how we were going to do each operation. "Start the drill by turning on the switch with your forefinger pressing the trigger." "Start the drill" is *what* we are going to do; "by pressing the trigger" is *how* we do it.

By breaking the operation down into the *what* and *how*, we are making it just that much easier for Chuck to remember what he is to do because in telling you what and how, he is getting two exposures to the operation. We are also clearing up any doubts he may have as to how something is done. When we were only telling him what we were doing, we were depending on his ability to observe to know how we were doing the operation. If he happened to miss something we were doing, then he would miss it himself when he told us what to do in Step 2 and when he did it himself in Step 3. If we are training him to use a spray gun and one of the operations calls for spreading a coat evenly but heavier in a certain spot, but failed to tell him that he should hold the gun as nearly perfectly still as possible and tilted up slightly, then he might not observe this at all. The "what and how" approach would cover this very well, however.

TELL THEM WHY

One final bit of detail that can be added is to tell the employees *why* we do the thing we are telling them how to do. To the clerk filling out the ledger sheet, we say, "Put the 25 in this space (What). The 25 was gotten from adding the sums of Row A and Row B (How). Row A and Row B are subtotals and when added together give us the grand total (Why)." In almost every case,

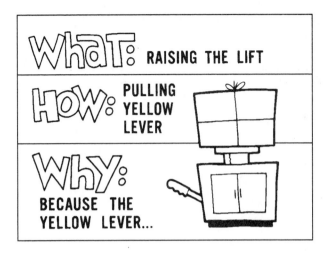

the why is important to building a better understanding and a better attitude toward the job. Employees who know why they are doing something are much better off because they can remember what to do longer and perhaps even improve on the job operation. If they don't know why, then they will do their work by rote. If they forget a step in the procedure, they have to be reminded because they cannot come up with a reason on their own. In the case of Chuck and the drill, if we include *why* in his training, he will know that the drill must remain turned on when it is withdrawn from the hole so as not to damage the sides. He will know that he must withdraw it slowly so as not to enlarge the hole. He will know to leave it running for a few seconds after it is out of the hole so as to clean the bit of metal shavings. Without the whys he will know to do these things but they may not seem very important to him. After a while, he may decide that some of the things are a waste of time and cut them out. The results may be ragged holes, damaged bits, filings left on the bit, etc.

All of these things can be included in the original job analysis chart if we are careful enough in planning the layout of the chart. It simply means that we will add columns to take care of the information we want to include. The chart may look like Figure 8.1. Note that by putting down the information in this

Figure 8.1   Job Analysis Chart
(Prepared for Instruction)

Step	Job Activity (What)	Procedure (How)	Reason (Why)

fashion, we have the training program practically prepared for us. We also have the means of simplifying or consolidating the material if we discover it is not hitting at the right level with the learner. Figure 8.2 shows the progression of steps in doing on-the-job training. There are some things to remember about these steps. First of all, the goal of this training is to get the information into the mind of the employee, since it is the mind that will be telling the hand (muscle) how and what to do. This is the reason why steps 3 and 5 are so important, though often left out. By having the employee tell the supervisor (or trainer) not only the steps of *what* to do, but the procedures of *how* and the considerations of *why* to do it a certain way, the steps are being embedded in the employee's mind. The trainer is also getting good feedback on the employee's understanding. Typically, the supervisor just tells the employee what to do, shows him or her, then asks, "Any questions?" If there aren't any, the supervisor says, "Okay, now you do it." The highest form of ensuring retention is having the learner say what she is doing before she does it. Just having her do it without saying anything reduces the chances for retention considerably.

Figure 8.2   Steps in Doing On-the-Job Training

Supervisor Tell: What How Why Step 1	Employee Tell: What How Why Step 3	Employee Tell: What How Why Step 5
Supervisor Do Step 2	Supervisor Do Step 4	Employee Do (Practice with Supervision) Step 6

OJT IN THE CLASSROOM

Let's add two considerations here. First, what happens when there are "hands-on" skills to be learned in what is otherwise a classroom situation? How is this handled? Second, what happens when we are in an OJT situation and there are several employees learning the same skill? Do we still use the same steps? Actually, we can follow almost the same procedures with several trainees as we do with one. The reason the process works in the first place is the amount of involvement and feedback we get from the learners. All we have to remember is not to lose that in our efforts to train more than one person. How does it work? Let's imagine that we have several people who have to learn something about a piece of equipment or a function on the computer or some manual skill. Since the learning and the memory are primarily in the mind, and memory is a function of what the *mind* does, we should keep the mind involved in the training. This means that there is accountability, there is response, and there is thinking going on among the learners.

We go through the same steps: 1) tell and show the employees what to do; 2) have an employee tell while we perform the actions; and, if the employee's "telling" is correct, 3) have an employee both tell and do the operation. We simply ask different employees to do the telling and the doing. We may stop in the middle of the telling, point to another employee, and say, "Okay, what comes next?" Even before this step is completed, we may do that again. During the "doing" stage, we do the same thing. In other words, we keep all the employees on guard, alert, and accountable by having them respond at random times. In no time at all, they will feel the accountability and be equally involved. While this probably will not be as completely effective as the one-on-one process is, it is a very good substitute and certainly better than a series of lectures or demonstrations or films. This technique is equally effective on the job or in the classroom. It is so much better than the usual way we do this kind of training, with the learners looking on while we talk and demonstrate and describe and warn, and then ask if there are any questions. Usually there aren't any questions, and perhaps a few people may even get to practice, but without going through the mental activities of saying anything. We've said it often in this book, and we say it again: "People remember what they say more than what they do, so we should get them saying things, not just doing things!"

CONCLUSION

Let's see what we have said about how to do on-the-job training. First, there must be self-preparation. Supervisors must be sure they are familiar with all of the information they are preparing to teach. They should study the material from the company manuals or specifications. They must study the techniques they will use in overcoming any barriers in communications. Finally, they should review the material they have put together in preparing the session they are going to instruct.

Then, there must be the preparing of the employee to be taught. The supervisor should put the employee at ease, using several ideas and approaches. The supervisor should open with a pleasant greeting then assure the employee that the learning will be accomplished. Finally, there is the necessity of creating interest and showing the employee what will be gained from the teaching–learning experience.

The instructor should be sure to stand or sit where the employee will be standing or sitting when the actual work operation is going on, with the employee facing the same way and located very close by. Remember, never face the person you are training. Always do the training from the same angle the employee will be working.

When the actual training starts, you should follow these procedures: *Demonstrate the process* (the instructor shows and tells). *Have the employee tell you* (employee tells, you do). Then, *have the employee do it* (employee tells, then does). In its fullest form, the training will look like this:

- Step 1. You tell *what* you are going to do and *how* you are going to do it, then *why* you did it, demonstrating each time.
- Step 2. The employee *tells you* what, how, and why, and you do what the employee says, provided it is the right procedure.
- Step 3. The employee tells you what, how, and why, and then *does it*, provided the employee has given you the right information.

One final consideration: Does it matter whether this is a new employee on an old job, or an old (experienced) employee on a new job? Note that the steps take into consideration only the procedures and will work in any of the cases mentioned. The preparation and size of the steps may differ considerably from one situation to the next, but the actual techniques used in the training will not change. If the preparation has been done well and the instructor follows the steps carefully, then learning will take place. That's what we were trying to accomplish all the time.

QUESTIONS FOR SMALL GROUP DISCUSSIONS

1. What are some of the things we need to do in preparing ourselves (as supervisors) for the training we are about to do with our employees?

2. What information from the personnel files might help us in reviewing for the training of specific individuals?

3. Read and study the following incident: Dave Olsen, a new foreman on the job, has the job of training several men, individually, in a new technique that is being introduced. He knows the

men by name but little else about their performance or ability. He approaches Ted to begin the new operation.

"Hello, Ted. How's it going?"

"Fine. I'm about over my cold, so I think I'll be back pretty regular now."

"That's fine. Sorry to hear you've been sick. I thought we'd get right on to some training this morning since I have several men to train."

"What's the training about?"

"The folks upstairs have got a new scheme they've worked out and want us to put into operation."

"Looks like they're always dreaming up something to mess up our work. I don't see what's wrong with what we're doing now."

"Well, I think you'll like this new method when you see how it works."

"I hope so. I have a lot of trouble learning new things."

"Maybe you won't have too much trouble, but you know I'm new at this, so I may not be the best teacher in the world."

Discuss the good and bad aspects of the above conversation from the standpoint of someone going to do some instructing.

4. What are some ways we can build interest and show personal advantages to the employee to be trained?

5. What is wrong with facing the employee when you are demonstrating how to do something?

6. Make up a training chart to show how you would train someone to perform an operation that requires tightening a plastic nut. The threads on the nut are delicate and must be only tight enough to prevent movement, not hold any pressure. The description of the operation at this stage reads, "Hold the nut loosely between the thumb and forefinger. Tighten until the nut is firm enough in the hand that it slips as pressure is applied lightly."

7. Pick some job you might be called on to train an employee to do. Break it down into small parts, then pick one of the parts and make a chart showing the steps in training a person to do this job. Be sure to show *what*, *how*, and *why* for each of the three steps in the training operation.

chapter 9

SPECIAL CONSIDERATIONS

Up until now we have been talking about situations where the employees are already on the job and we are trying to train them to do something better or different. We have assumed they knew a little about the job and the equipment but needed some help in a particular area of the work. But this isn't always the case. There are times when the job is entirely new and the employee is experienced on some job other than this one. There are times when the employee is completely new and needs to be trained on a job that has been around for a long time. Sometimes there are situations where the job and the employee are *both* new. Finally, of course, there are variations in between these situations. Let's look at some of the problems that might arise and see where what we have already said will fit and where something different will have to be used.

NEW EMPLOYEE, OLD JOB

Probably the most common situation is where there is a replacement coming in to do the job someone else has been doing. How do we handle this? First of all, let's repeat what we have said before several times. The basic three-step process for the actual training will remain the same for *all the situations* we mentioned in the preceding paragraph. The things that will change will be in the preparation stages, not in the actual training. In the case we have under consideration here, we might break down the job into smaller bits, but the actual training would look very much the same. Even some of the earlier stages of preparation will be the same as they would if the employee had been around for some time.

For example, the job analysis chart would be the same for anyone, new or old. In this chart we look at the *job*, not at the employee. We break it down into small enough steps that we are able to identify each action, each movement the employee will have to go through. We become so familiar with the job that we can specify where the hands, the eyes, the material being worked with, and the equipment will be at any given time. We know what comes first, what comes next, and what comes last. Since we take our training from this, we know that the training will look the same regardless of who is being trained.

Another thing that will be the same will be the objectives. When we prepare the objectives that tell us what the employee will be able to do when the training is over, they should look the same for anyone taking the training. Even in a case where a new person required more intensive training and several sessions were required, the end product of the training would be the same because the objective of the complete training program should be to have the employee performing the job properly. The only difference would be in how far back the training starts. The objectives must take into account what is a realistic goal to shoot at and just how much the employee can learn to do in the time allowed. If the employee is new, the training may take longer because there may be many things that have to be learned in the way of procedures, terms, definitions, etc. By all means, *the objectives should take this into consideration*. In the case of the new person, the training may have to be divided into several sections, with different time assignments given. It may be that the training will have to be spread out over a number of different days. If these things do occur, then *each* of these training efforts should have its own set of objectives. This may take a little longer to prepare but will actually make the training much easier to do once the objectives have been set. At each session the employee will know what is to be accomplished, and the supervisor will be able to tell if the goal of that particular effort has been achieved by looking at the objective and seeing if the employee can, for this session, do what the objective says the employee is supposed to be able to do.

Lack of Information

One problem that may exist with a new employee is the lack of information on the person's abilities, personality, likes and dislikes, etc. We don't know much about the employee's attitudes toward the job, the company, and training. As we have seen, this kind of information is helpful in putting together the training program. Without it we may end up going too fast or too slow. We may find ourselves using words or phrases that are obnoxious or unfamiliar. We may cause the employee to become resentful of us or the company and not even know why.

How do we find out about these things? First of all, let's note that we aren't trying to "spoon feed" the employee. The employee is an adult and supposedly came to learn the job and perform it satisfactorily. *We* have a right to expect this much and must operate on that basis. What we are trying to do is apply a little common sense and in the process do a better job of training. With this in mind, we find ourselves simply looking for ways to learn as much as possible about the individual so we can teach as much as possible of what it is we want that individual to have. We look for this information anywhere we think we can find it. It needn't be a completely "hit-or-miss" proposition, though. There are sources that are available to us that will help greatly, and we should use them as often as possible

For example, the *employment* interview that took place at the time the employee was hired should be a good source of valuable information. Many times this gets tucked away in the

employment files and is not even used by the supervisor on the job. But remember, this is probably the most comprehensive single interview the employee will ever have while with the company. Here the employee was tested—perhaps by a professional psychologist—with a number of different kinds of tests. Perhaps there were aptitude tests that tell us how well we can expect the person to learn. There may have been personality tests or work preference tests or any number of tests that give us helpful information. In fact, these tests may give us more than we could learn about the employee even after several months of working for us. This doesn't mean that we should rely solely on the tests and not use our own judgment. Rather, it means that *we should use our judgment in understanding and interpreting the test results.*

But the employee's hiring interview gives us more than just test results; it tells us many personal things about the employee. We can find out how many children the employee has, what their ages are, and perhaps other things about them. We can find out what the person's hobbies, outside interests, and maybe even "hopes and aspirations" for the future are, if these were covered in the initial interview. We can find out why the employee chose to come with this company. We can look at the employee's references and see if the recommendations are very favorable or just the routine "I-have-known-this-person-for-ten-years-and-find-him-to-be-of-reputable-character" kind.

It should be noted that we aren't talking about the regular personnel file. We are talking about the file that was made up when the employee came in to seek employment the first time. It includes the results from whatever initial testing was done, the forms the employee filled out, and any answers that were given orally during the personal contact. It may include any assessment that was made of the employee at the time of the interview. For some reason, this information is seldom kept with the regular personnel records that follow employees from assignment to assignment. The supervisor should look for this, even if training isn't under consideration, because it contains valuable information that may affect future promotions and wage increases. Some of this information might even explain an employee's deficiencies and help us put the employee back on the right track.

There are other sources, though, and one we have already mentioned is valuable—the employee's training file. Here are basic facts—previous training, possibly the results that were achieved during training, and perhaps other valuable facts. From the training file, we can find out the "hard" facts. We can tell just so much from this, though, and no more. The facts aren't interpreted for us, nor will we find reasons for motivation or the lack of it. The fact that she went to school at a certain place ten years ago doesn't tell us how much of what she learned is still part of her action and reaction. The fact that he has had five years of experience on another job doesn't tell us that he was good or bad at that job or that he will necessarily be good or bad at the one he is getting ready to train for. Here again we find the need for using our own judgment in interpreting the things that appear on the records. We have to be careful not to read anything into the record that isn't there, but at the same time we should try to be as perceptive as possible so as to glean as much as we can from what is available.

Planning Stage Will Differ

When we are training someone who is new on the job, we should make most of our changes during the planning stage.

After we have done whatever we can to find out about the new employee from the various personnel records, we put this to work in planning how we will handle the training. Using the same plans as before so far as *setting objectives* and doing the *job analysis* are concerned, we see what adjustments we have to make for the new person. If we have found that the new person appears to have a special skill in certain areas and weaknesses in others, we plan accordingly. If the record shows that the employee was hard to talk to during the hiring interview, we make special notes for the "putting at ease" step (we make note of hobbies, family background, etc.). If the record shows experience on a similar operation, we make a note to use this during the part of our introduction when we are assuring the employee that learning this new skill will be just as easy. In other words, we make note of those things that put us a few steps ahead in making new employees feel at ease and giving them confidence in their ability to learn the task we are going to talk about.

Another phase of the planning stage that will differ is the breakdown of the small steps to be used in the training. We may want to make them smaller because of the lack of experience. We may want to make notes to ourselves on places where the steps can be made larger if we discover the employee is learning faster than we had expected. We will want to leave ourselves space to answer some questions that will help us later on, such as likes and dislikes, strengths and weaknesses, previous successes and failures in training ("I never was able to learn that!"), and anything else we think will help us in our future training efforts with this employee. As we do the actual training, we may discover, of course, that some of the apparent strengths and weaknesses are the results of lack of training, not lack of ability. If we suspect this, a note to ourselves will remind us to check out our suspicions at a later date.

The Training Is the Same

After our preplanning stage is finished and we start the actual steps in the training, we will find that the things done will look pretty much the same as any other training effort done on the job. The steps may be smaller, the words may be simpler, the getting started stage may be a little longer, but the step-by-step process will still be the same basic activities we went through before. It will be: Step 1, we tell, we do; step 2, employee tells, we do; step 3, employee tells, employee does. No matter what experience (or lack of it) the employee might have, we follow this same procedure. In each case, we expand it to include *how* and *why*. When we are through, the employee will have seen what to do, how to do it, and why it is done this way. We will have *seen the employee do it* and *heard the employee tell us* why it is done this way. (It is easy to see where this could be very valuable in the future. "I don't see why we have to do it this way" can be answered with, "What was it you told me during the training?")

NEW JOB, "OLD" EMPLOYEE

While we often think that the most difficult part of the training task is to work with someone who is brand new on the job and knows nothing about the terminology or equipment, many times it is even more difficult to take someone who has been doing a job a certain way for many, many years and train that person to do a completely new method, on an entirely new piece of equipment. Since we strike at the very roots of the employee's job security (the ability to do the job), we may often get strong reactions. But the job of training the experienced person on a new operation is not impossible and can be a very pleasant experience. There are some things we need to remember, and if we do, the training job should go smoothly enough.

First of all, *it isn't completely true that people resist change*. It is more correct to say that people resist *being changed*. Employees buy *new* cars, *new* clothes, *new* houses, and all kinds of new possessions. Certainly one reason they work is to make these changes from the old to the new. So it isn't enough to say that people just don't like to change. Note something about their buying habits: They buy at the same store ("You just can't beat their clothes!"); they buy the same kind of car (and almost fight to prove it is the best). But they do sometimes buy from a different store and they do sometimes buy different kinds of cars. One of the main reasons they make these changes is that they think there is *some advantage to them in making the change.* And this sums up the approach we must take in training these experienced employees in something new: We must show that there is some advantage to them in making this change.

In the last chapter, we pointed out that it was important to show the employee the *personal advantage* of the training we were about to do. In the case of retraining an experienced employee, this is certainly more than nice—it is essential. Since the employee's security may be threatened, we must make a special effort to show that there will actually be personal gain as a result of this change. Of course, we should be sure to be honest with the employees and if they are being phased out of work for some reason, it may be the best time to tell them. But the case we are talking about here is one where the employee should have many more years of productive time with the company. The only problem is that the particular *operation* the employee is now doing is being changed and we want to make it possible for this employee to reach maximum production on the new operation as quickly as possible. Because of this, training is being done. When we convince people of this, we will be well on our way to relieving their minds and restoring their sense of security.

How do we convince them of our objectives? Perhaps the best way is the same as we discussed earlier—put them at ease by telling them the advantage of learning how to do the new operation. At the same time, let them know very quickly that we are sure they can learn the new skills required without any trouble. The advantages should already be obvious. The old job will disappear, and only those who can do the new one will have satisfactory work arrangements. But this is too blunt. This simply says, "Learn it or you're out of a job."

A better way is to show Harry that he is the first to be given the chance to learn the job because he is a valuable employee. "The company wants you to learn this job first so that we can use all of your valuable experience in the new operation." Or we might want to tell Harry, "We would like for you to learn this so you can help us train the rest of the group." If we hope to get immediate results from the new operation, we might try something like, "The sooner we get some of the experts like you trained, the sooner we can start to get some of the benefits from this new equipment." The prospect of competition may bring out the challenge aspect of the new operation. "You know that the Ajax Company is already using this equipment, and I know you can do a better job than they can." Any of these approaches should work, providing what we say is true and not just an effort to shunt Harry to some kind of shelf job. (Not that this might not have to be done sometime; it's just that we may find our words coming back to haunt us one day when Harry starts to ask for all those advantages we promised him.)

Preplanning Is Still Essential

Even though the employee may have considerable experience, we still cannot overlook the importance of preplanning for the training we are about to do. In fact, the planning may well save us considerable time in the long run. As we study the job analysis, we may discover many items that are similar to those being performed by the employees in their present assignment. Now it becomes a matter of finding those things that are similar and those that are different and planning our training accordingly. If we don't make an effort to find this out ahead of time, we may find that our training effort becomes boring to the employees because we spend too much time on things they already know. On the other hand, even though the employees already know certain portions of the job, we should be sure not to just bypass that part of the job in our training. This may cause them to get the wrong concept of what is supposed to be done and when it is supposed to be done. If we can describe the portion already known without confusing the employees, then we can do this. If we think the employees may still get mixed up, we may have them just demonstrate that they can do it by telling them to put this part in at this time. "At this point you follow the same procedures you have been using on the other machine. How about going through that once and see how it goes." It is always better to have them go through the operation than for you to do it yourself, because this will give you a chance to see if they really do know how to perform the work satisfactorily.

One thing we will want to do is *be sure we don't take too much for granted* as we plan the training. Be careful not to start thinking, "Well, I'm sure Alice knows this after all these years, so I won't bore her with these details." Those "boring details" may be just the thing Alice needs to get her production up in a hurry. Also, in our planning we may want to check the terminology and phrases we use because sometimes the new equipment may use the same words, but with slightly different meanings. If this is the case, the word-drill exercise we talked about earlier will be essential here.

Again, we note that once the preplanning has been done and a suitable set of objectives has been agreed upon, the actual training will look very much like the other we have talked about. The only differences will be in the size of the steps and in the length of time we spend on each item. If experience is really an asset to this job, the training will cover more ground in bigger bits. Also, the employees may be able to take longer training at any one time since they don't have to learn everything from the very beginning. They may not require as much time to absorb the training as new employees may.

There are other considerations we might look at, such as the new person on the job and the older person being trained again to improve production. In both cases, however, the procedures are the same: Look at the job analysis, plan for the individual and the individual's needs (or groups of individuals with the same kinds of backgrounds or problems), then follow the steps already outlined. With proper planning, realistic objectives, and step-by-step training, the results should be perfectly satisfactory, regardless of the experience of the individual or the length of time the job has been around.

EMPLOYEE INVOLVEMENT IN TRAINING DECISIONS

Another factor that needs to be considered here is getting the employees involved in some of the training decisions. This is especially true of new employees since they're going to be participating in so much training early in their careers. If we can get them "training conscious" at the beginning of their employment, they'll "think training" the rest of their employment lives. Just what does this mean? The most obvious thing is that they will come to understand that their job performance and their evaluation and their future are very dependent upon training. If this is emphasized early enough, they will keep it for the rest of their time with us. The advantages are severalfold, and there are some disadvantages, mostly self-inflicted, as we'll see.

If we can get the employees in the habit of looking for areas where they need training, it will help us decide when training is necessary and certainly improve the reception of the training, as far as the employees are concerned. Not being able to do something ought automatically to trigger thoughts of training in the minds of supervisor and subordinate alike. If, in the orientation portion of employee training, we are able to stress the importance of training to the extent that we will have employees recognizing that they need training because there is something they can't do, we'll be far ahead. Instead of our waiting for them to fail on the job, get a bad appraisal or review of some kind, and then deciding that training would have helped, the training now comes first. The employees are assigned a task to do, find they don't know how, and then immediately come to us for help. It is a measure of the maturity of both the supervisor and the employees if they feel that they can come to us for training and that it is to their advantage and not a sign of a flaw in their employment. To carry this further, we can also have them looking for *training priorities*. They see several things they are weak on, where training will help, but realize that they can't get all the training at once, so they make the decision for us as to what they feel is the order of training. They make a recommendation as to the place where training will have the most return or payoff. We'll have to help them in these decisions, of course, and we have the right to influence their thoughts, but for the most part we'll discover that they know a great deal about where the training is needed and when.

Along this same line, we can also get them involved early in their careers in looking for areas where change in procedures or policies will help. This means that instead of seeing the need for further training, they'll now be looking at the job in terms of how to best do it. If we let them not only know that they have an opportunity to make suggestions for training—in more than just some kind of "suggestion plan"— but also see that we take their suggestions seriously, they'll also look for training when they have trouble doing the job and they'll look to see if the job could be done better some other way. When this starts to happen, even though there will be times when we can't use the suggestions, we'll start to get much more commitment from them as far as day-to-day work is concerned. Since this will stem from a deficiency of some kind on their part, we should still look at areas where training might be the solution. However, both we and the employees soon learn that training people to do a job that's poorly designed is simply promoting poor performance, not improving performance.

The next advantage in getting the employees to look for training early in their career activities is that they can begin to do some of their own training. In fact, if we let them know that there is a process of training, done a step at a time, and they understand this process, they can soon become trainers themselves. This is often best done with older, more experienced employees, but doesn't have to be limited to just them. We should emphasize the importance of the training assignment, however. The worst possible way to have training is to make training a burden, a low-prestige job, or something that the least experienced person on the job does. Those selected to do the training should be trained in how to do it, should be called trainers while they're doing it, and should be recognized when they do it. We might even list them on the bulletin board as the trainers for the quarter, or have a newsletter that is distributed just to those doing the training. This will give them some prestige and let them know that the organization thinks the training is important. It's always significant to employees when they find out somebody thinks they are important, or that their job is important. This is one of the easy ways of accomplishing a quick bit of positive reinforcement!

The final advantage we want to discuss is one that could bring about a disadvantage if we aren't careful. If, in the very early days of training the employees, we give them an understanding of the step-by-step process of doing on-the-job training, these employees will more likely push their supervisors to do good training. If we insist that we want them to get the kind of training talked about in this book, the employees will usually urge their supervisors to give them this kind of training. If we explain the urgency of having the supervisor or trainer get them involved, when the supervisor trains them just by explaining and showing, but without involvement, the employee will say something like, "Would it be all right if I went through the process once by telling you, before you mark me down as having had the training?" If we tell the new employees, as we are giving them orientation, "Don't ever let a person train you and leave you without asking you to tell them what you're supposed to do," we'll get some good training, whether the supervisors intended to do this kind of training or not. However, it is now that we may find our disadvantage: There will be some supervisors who will be unhappy with us when their employees start to question their training techniques. Evidence is strong that many supervisors don't use the steps talked about here and that the results of their kind of training are poor. Essentially, they tell, show, ask if there are any questions, and then say to the employee, "Okay, you do it." Never once do they do anything to teach the procedures and safety considerations. This is obviously poor training. These kinds of supervisors, who reject good training procedures, are also unhappy when their employees ask to be allowed to say something during the training. It may well be that this is not a disadvantage and may result in our getting better trainers—under duress—out of our supervisors.

CONCLUSION

Up until now we've been talking about situations where the employees are already on the job and we are trying to train them to do something better or more correctly. This isn't always the case. There are times when the job is entirely new and the employee is experienced on some job other than this one, or the employee is completely new and needs training on a job that has been around for a long time. Sometimes both the job and the employee are new. So how do we deal with these special situations? The procedures are the same. Use the job analysis chart and plan for the individual's needs; then follow the steps we've already outlined. The only changes will be in the *preparation* stages, not in the actual training.

QUESTIONS FOR SMALL GROUP DISCUSSIONS

1. What special considerations should be given to the planning activities when we are training a new person on a job that has been in existence for several years?

2. What are some of the ways we can get more information on an employee who has just come to work for us and is now to be trained?

3. Thinking about your own situation, what kind of records are available to you as a possible source of information that will help in planning your training activities?

4. What problems might appear when we start to retrain a person who has been doing a job that is now being phased out?

5. Discuss ways of rebuilding a sense of security in an individual who is being trained on a new job because the one he has been doing for a long time is now obsolete.

6. What are some of the ways we can overcome the employee's natural resistance to being changed to a new job?

7. Discuss some instance where you have had to train someone who resented having to learn a new job. How could you have improved the job you did?

chapter 10

WHAT TO DO WHEN THE TRAINING IS OVER

In Chapter 6 we discussed the importance of setting objectives that stated just exactly what we wanted the employee to be able to do at the end of the training period. Now that we have seen the steps in setting up the training and carrying it out, let's see how we *evaluate the objectives* we set earlier. Since we said that the objectives were to show us what the employee should be able to do, the measure of the objective should be simply finding out if the employee really can do it. In the three steps we have taken to do the training, we have actually seen the employee perform the task and explain the reason for doing it. We have, then, seen the objective met. If not, then the training was not effective, or perhaps the planning was not done very well. In either case, the objective was not reached, and we know it, so the objective served the purpose of telling us we fell short, whether or not it tells us *where* we went wrong. Our problem now is to find the trouble and make the necessary corrections.

EVALUATING TRAINING

There is always the possible chance that something about the training does not allow us to let the employees perform *exactly* as they will be doing on the job. In this case, we should have set our objective for a satisfactory job at the real work situation, not just at the end of the training. This means, though, that we will not be able to determine whether or not the objective has been reached until we observe the employees at work on the regular job. There is one way we may be able to avoid this, and that is by taking them to the job site immediately after the training is over and letting them perform certain operations. For instance, the objective may have been for the employees "to be able to begin an operation and completely cycle the equipment." If this is the objective, and we have not been able to use the actual equipment in the training or for some reason have not been able to have the training completely resemble the job environment, we now take an employee to the work location to perform the operation for us. We wait for the proper time on the equipment, then let the employee begin an operation and cycle the equipment. This way the action should not interfere with the normal operation of the equipment, and we will be measuring the employee under actual working conditions.

It may even be necessary for us to wait for several hours or even a few days until the employees can completely demonstrate that they have achieved all of the objectives. If this is the case, we should be sure to see that we check them out at the earliest possible moment. There is no reason to lose the benefits of the entire training effort because we haven't had the chance to make the final performance check on the job. If we haven't checked out the employees on meeting the objectives, we should be sure not to go ahead and record that they have completed the training. We may find ourselves having to remove an entry from an employee's training record because he really can't do the job. If there is some reason why we can't check to see if the objectives have been met, we should avoid the temptation to say, "Well, I'm sure you know this all right. I'll just let it go and show you have satisfactorily completed the training." We will be embarrassed when we have to go back and say, "I'm taking this out of your training record because we have to go through the training again."

Not a Mystery

Objectives shouldn't be thought of as things that are very difficult and almost impossible to evaluate. There is no mystery to
testing to see if the objectives have been met. It is simply a matter of being sure the objectives were stated correctly in the first
place. Let's refresh our thinking for a moment and see what we
mean by "stating them correctly." Note the two objectives listed
here, each talking about the same training requirements:

1. The purpose of the course is to give the employee a good
   understanding of plant equipment.
2. At the end of the training, the employee will be able to identify the following pieces of equipment and explain their functions (list of equipment follows).

Now try to make up a test to see if the employee has met the
objectives as stated in the two examples. What would you have
the employee do in the first case? If three people read this, there
would probably be three different opinions. But look at the second case. There is no room for disagreement here. The test is
simply to have the employee identify the pieces of equipment
listed and explain the function of each.

This process could be repeated over and over again, and the
results would be the same. "Be able to recognize good and bad
spot welds." "Be able to specify the proper forms to use in each
type of force reporting." "Be able to identify unsafe working procedures." "Be able to give the proper secretarial telephone
response for the following types of calls." "Be able to list the exact
tools required and be able to draw these tools from the store-
room." *The tests for these are actually contained in the objectives themselves.* It becomes only a matter of having the employees demonstrate that they can do what the objectives say they should be able
to do. In most cases, even someone who isn't familiar with the
job at all would be able to tell if the objective had been met.

RECORDING THE TRAINING

From this we ought to be able to see that if the objectives are
written correctly, the testing of these objectives is probably the

easiest part of the job. But there is still another step that is important. We should pay close attention to the *recording of the training*.
From our earlier chapters we saw the importance of having the
kind of training the individual has had recorded in permanent
personnel training files. We saw how important it was to us to
be able to go to the record and see that the employee had successfully (or unsuccessfully) completed certain training programs. We found out that it was very valuable to us to be able to
know that the employee had been given training on this same
job at some other time, especially when we are troubled because
the employee's performance is below standard right now.

More and more organizations are finding it important to
record the training efforts. With the various kinds of certification
such as OSHA, NRC, EEOC, and EPA are concerned, or even
customer certification, all these things are important to have on
file. Even though there doesn't seem to be any present need for a
particular training record, the more records we keep, the safer
we are in the long run if our training is ever called to question.
The training records become a part of documentation in case
there is ever a question as to whether a person was properly
trained for safety, health, or other things that might involve
some kind of government regulations. It doesn't take very long
to record the training; therefore it is time well spent in case we
have a need to refer to it later.

Training records are a very valuable part of the total picture
of a worker, and if we fail to keep these records up-to-date, we
are presenting only part of the person to those who look at the
records. If promotion or demotion is being considered, then the
records should tell all of the story. When we go to "put the
employee at ease," we ought to be able to talk in an up-to-date
fashion regarding the employee's previous training, rather than
discover that we are looking at old and incorrect information.

"You know, Charlie, I don't see why you haven't had this
kind of training before."
"Oh, I have. Just last year."
(Now where do we go?)

For every company (and every department sometimes),
there is a different form and way to record the training information. But they all should lend themselves to one thing: They

should provide space not only to show what training has been done, but also *what training is anticipated*. Ideally, these records should show the step-by-step training program for each employee. This way, anyone looking at the records can tell at a glance just where the employee has been and where he is going. As each training exercise is completed, it is noted in records, showing the date and the person responsible for the training. At the same time this notation is made, the supervisor can make at least a mental note as to when the best time would be for the next step in the training program. A good training record will show the best times for the training. For example, "Within the first three months . . . not before six months of experience . . . should precede training step number four . . . ." This way, supervisors can set a timetable for themselves and the employees so they won't forget to do the training at the best time for the employees and the job.

CERTIFICATION—IMPORTANT, BUT WITH HAZARDS

So far we've seen that many things make up good training. The design, the preparation of both the trainer and the trainee, the timing and the location, and finally, the training itself, all combine to make the training successful. Many organizations are making efforts to become certified for their training. Certification programs such as the International Standards Organization's Quality Standards (ISO 9000) have very stringent requirements for documented job procedures (such as discussed in the chapters on "Analysis"), and for job training. This makes adherence to the things discussed in this book all the more important. If the procedures are followed as shown, the certification should be easy. However, there are some problems.

Unfortunately, most certification programs, by their own admission, do not have a good way of determining just how good the training actually is. Most programs look more at the amount of training, the topics trained on, and the measurement processes (testing), rather than the actual techniques used in the training. Many successful organizations have a way of ensuring that good training is done, by conducting a "Train-the-Trainer" program *for both the trainers and the trainees*. The trainer training is not on the topics or skills being done on the job, but on how to do on-the-job training. By training the potential trainees, the organization can be sure that the trainees will be more anxious to see good training, since they are told not to let the supervisor record the training if the proper procedures were not used.

This same thing is true for many government regulations, where training is required for government approval of one kind or another. For example, to be a qualified trainer in the nuclear industry, many days of learning how to train are required, but none of the requirements is able to specify how good the training is. It stands to reason, though, that any organization interested in certification for any reason would want the training to be the best. The conclusion: "Don't document bad training."

FOLLOW-UP—THE FINAL KEY TO SUCCESS

Unfortunately, we sometimes stop right here. We have done our planning well, after analyzing the job and the person doing the job; we have gone through the steps of the training and checked the employee's performance against the objectives set in advance; we have duly recorded the training and performance results in the permanent files after we are sure the employee has properly met the objectives. *But our job is not yet complete.* We must remember the final key to success—the follow-up.

Employees forget what they have been trained to do, and although the method we have been describing is designed to make the training as lasting as possible, there is always the possibility that the employee may end up not doing the job correctly. It may be that when the employee gets back on the job, a distraction will result in the job being done incorrectly. The day-to-day routine will sometimes get the employees back in the habit of performing the task in a sloppy manner or make them leave out important parts of their work. Unless we follow up, we may not find this out until it is too late. If we make a check shortly after things are back to normal and find the work isn't being done correctly, we will have a chance to change whatever is causing the employee to perform poorly. If we wait too long, the chances of finding the source of the trouble are pretty poor.

The follow-up need not be a formal training routine. It can be a brief visit to the work site in which we ask George to demonstrate the things we taught in the training session. It might include a look at George's production sheet to see how he is doing. If his production is no better than before the training, then either the training was poor or something else is influencing George's behavior. If things look too bad we may want to

make another work analysis sheet on George to see just how he is going about his job. We may want to talk to him and see if he has any ideas why his work is not up to standard. A remark from him like, "Nobody else around here does it the right way," may be the clue to more major training needs. On the other hand, something like, "I still don't see why it has to be done the way you showed me," can give us valuable information on the employee's attitude. It also shows a weakness in one step in our training activities—the "why" phase.

The chances are that we won't run into these types of problems, though. What we will probably find is that the employee is doing everything right with the exception of a few minor details. It is these small items that make the follow-up so valuable. We watch George go through the operation, look at his production record, note the few things that could be improved, and then decide whether or not more training is required. The chances are good that we won't have to do much more than mention to George where his shortcomings are, and he will do the rest. Of course, if he is too far wrong, then by all means we will want to set up a time and place to go through the regular steps of on-the-job training we have been talking about in this book. Since by now we have memorized the steps in the training, we might be able to stop him right on the job as soon as we see he is having trouble and go through a short session with him right there. This is always effective and can be very timesaving as well. By the way, a good training record should include a place to note that a follow-up has been done, and the results of that follow-up. A place simply labeled "remarks" may be good enough.

NOW WHERE?

There are no more steps. The job of training has been done, and you have made the necessary entries and done your follow-up. It would be nice to think that there is no more training to do, but that isn't the case. As we post the training we have just done in the employee's record, we note that she will soon be or perhaps is ready for the next session. We note, too, that this isn't the only employee we have who needs training. There are others who need the same training this employee just got, and there are others who need other training. So the job of training is never-ending. It is a part of the supervisor's job, and just as making supervisory decisions never ceases, neither does the work of training. Much, much earlier in the book, we pointed out that when the supervisor undertakes a training job, that is the most important thing to be done right at that moment. By this supervisors should be measured and by this they should be rewarded. After all, supervisors expect their employees to do well—the same rule applies to them as well.

It would not be completely honest to close this book without mentioning something about "reinforcement." *It is no surprise to us that people do those things that are rewarding to them.* They are more likely to repeat those things for which they receive the most reward. "Reward" in this case doesn't necessarily mean a tangible reward, such as money or promotion. It also means such things as praise or recognition or acceptance. When we are talking about "follow-up" and "evaluating training," we should ask ourselves just why it is that the employee will want to do the job correctly. What "reinforcement" is there on the job to make *doing it correctly* rewarding? Here are three questions that have to be answered in order to see whether or not the training will "take":

1. Is there something on the job that will reward the *wrong* behavior?
2. Is there something on the job that will punish the *right* behavior?
3. Is there something on the job that will reward the *right* behavior?

If we come up with the wrong answers to these questions, we're in trouble. We can't predict much success for the training, no matter how good it has been. Let's consider them one at a time.

Suppose we have set a standard for typists of no corrections before the third paragraph. It is a reasonable requirement to some since it keeps the reader from seeing errors early in the letter, and people are more tolerant when they see errors down in the body of the letter than when they see them in the date or address. By the time the error shows up in the second paragraph, the reader is more engrossed in the content and worries less about the appearance of the letter. (Or so the theory goes.)

But there is a small crisis, and the boss wants the letters out in a hurry. The typist makes an error in the address, makes a very neat correction, and finishes the letter in a hurry. The boss is happy, and the typist is rewarded for the wrong behavior.

We might take another example: The organization is very safety conscious. "Take time to be safe: It's the best way," the posters say, all over the walls. One rule is that no employee should stand on anything but an approved ladder. These ladders are tagged, checked, and stored in the supply closet at one end of the work area. A particular employee is somewhat lazy and doesn't like to make the trip to the far end of the work area every time there is a need for getting something off the shelf. There is a small, boxlike protrusion in the equipment that is very sturdy *and* conveniently located under the shelving. The boss has criticized this employee for being slow, and when there was a need for something from the shelf and the employee returned with it in a hurry, the boss was complimentary of the speed with which it was obtained, not knowing the ladder was not being used. The result was that the employee was rewarded for the wrong behavior, and there isn't much chance that the employee will use the ladder the next time there is a need to get something from the shelf.

But how can we "punish the *right* behavior"? Simply by causing the employee to lose something valuable, like time or energy, or by causing the employee to be criticized for doing something correctly, even if this criticism comes from a peer. Take a simple case where we've worked very diligently to get a salesperson to print in all caps on the sales slip. The employee has trouble printing, and it takes a while to accomplish the task. When there isn't much of a crowd, the employee can print without causing undue hardship on anyone, but when there is a crowd and there is only one cash register, and several salespeople are waiting to get to the cash register but are prevented because of a slow printer, there is going to be punishment for the correct (and slow) behavior. The other salespeople are keeping their customers waiting, so they make unkind remarks; the waiting customers make a remark or two; and the poor employee who is having trouble printing is missing sales and thinks some unkind thoughts about the "lousy system." This may sound like an exaggeration, but it happens often in many organizations.

Finally, what about a reward for doing the job correctly? Is there one? Suppose the employee does the job correctly time after time after time—what then? Further, suppose the employee does the job correctly most of the time but then messes up on a few occasions. Does anything different happen? If not, then there is no reward for doing it correctly, at least no more than for doing it incorrectly. If doing it right takes more effort or takes longer or requires more thought, but nothing ever happens to reinforce this, then we can't expect the good behavior to continue indefinitely.

What has all this got to do with training? Simply this: We said that we train because an employee isn't doing the job or isn't doing it well enough or is doing it incorrectly. *If we are going to train, then we'd better make sure that the deficiency isn't caused by the reinforcement problems we've talked about here.* It would be nice if all the employees would work well, just because they wanted to do what is right. But this won't always be the case, and we all know that. But most will want to do what is right if we will just give them a little encouragement. We should make sure that we are giving them every chance they need to do the job correctly. This is especially true after they have been trained. If we want to get the best evaluation of our training—that is, the most accurate—we should be sure to provide the best possible situation for doing the work correctly on the job. The best training in the world isn't likely to overcome very bad working conditions. But even fair training has a good chance of succeeding when there is the proper reinforcement of the correct behavior. Just think of the chances of success when there is excellent training and plenty of reinforcement on the job.

IMMEDIATE USE IS IMPORTANT

One thing that we all have in common is our outstanding ability to forget. Everyone forgets rapidly, and most of our forgetting is done in a matter of hours. Perhaps the bulk of our forgetting is done within the first three days of learning something. If the training has been such that the employees have used their minds as well as their heads, they will have quite a bit of their learning still with them at the end of the three days. However, we should be certain that they get a chance to use what they've learned as quickly as possible. We can enhance their remembrance greatly by letting them perform the tasks they've learned immediately on the "real" job. The use should be beyond just practice; it should be doing something that is a part of the regular production activity. If it is perceived of as only "practice," it will have less significance and still be thought of as "training," which it is, of course. On the other hand, if they are actually doing something for which they'll be accountable, something that will be seen and measured and used, their commitment will be greater.

This tells us something about the timing of our training, too. *If we know that they will not be using the information and skill soon, it makes better sense to wait to train them until they're ready to apply what they learn.* We can't keep training in "cold storage" until needed. It also suggests that they ought to be expected to do on the job what they are learning, in just the same way they are learning it. We should avoid, at all costs, training them in a procedure that is out-of-date so that they will be told, "That's the way we used to do it, but you'll be doing it with these modifications." This doesn't happen too often, but *never* would be a better record. *The whole point is to see that they get a chance to apply the skills they've just learned, as soon as possible, in the way they've learned it, in a real situation.* The likelihood of them continuing to do it the way we trained them will be much greater under these conditions.

CONCLUSION

What do we do now? We want to find out how well the training was done. How do we do it? We must evaluate the employees who have been trained as to how well they meet the objectives we set. In the three steps we have taken to do the training, we have actually *seen* the employees perform the tasks and explain the reasons for doing them. We have, in fact, seen the objectives met! Another thing that is very important is that we must pay close attention to the *recording* of the training. Training records are a very valuable part of the total picture of any employee. But we must not stop there. The final key to success is the follow-up.

It need not be a formal procedure, but it should include at least a brief observation of the employee performing the job under actual working conditions.

No more steps; the job of training has been completed, the necessary entries have been made, and we have done our follow-up. There's nothing left to do, right? Wrong! The same employee will soon be ready for the next phase of training, and there will be others who need the same or other training. So the training job never ends. It is a part of the supervisor's job and, just as making supervisory decisions never ceases, neither does the work of training!

QUESTIONS FOR SMALL GROUP DISCUSSIONS

1. Discuss the meaning of the statement, "The tests for these (objectives) are actually contained in the objectives themselves."

2. Make up an objective for a short teaching session you might be involved in and then state how you would test to see if this objective has been met.

3. What are some of the ways good training records will help us in planning our training?

4. Describe your own training records and explain how they are similar and how they differ from the requirements set forth in this chapter.

5. What else should be in a training record besides the training that has already been done?

6. What are some of the things that might cause the employee to do a poor job, even after the training has been given?

7. What are some of the things we should look for when we do our follow-up inspection?

chapter 11

TRAINING FOR CAREER ADVANCEMENT

In this chapter we want to deal with a special problem that exists in all kinds of jobs: training people so that they can move ahead in their organization. We are primarily concerned here with the relatively low-skilled employees, although advancement should not be thought of as a problem only with this group. We want to talk about several different aspects, including problems encountered, means of motivation, differences in attitudes, and the importance of follow-up and evaluation. First, let's just open up the subject by looking at it from various angles.

DEFINING THE PROBLEM

"Upward mobility" has several connotations. Some see it in a very limited scope, referring to those who are from the "disadvantaged" sector who have minimal skills and minimal education. Others think of it in the broadest terms, referring to anyone moving up from any job in the organization. Others find a happy medium and refer to those who are at the lower end of the skills level but not necessarily classified as disadvantaged. For our purposes, we will think most of the time of the latter group, so when we refer to upward mobility, you should think about a person who hasn't much to offer in the way of trained skills above the job now assigned, but someone whom we would like to see get a better job in the organization—a better job being defined as one that requires more skill than the employee now has, and one that pays more money for that skill.

What is the problem at this level? There are several aspects to the problem. Not all of them are simple, but it's worth mentioning some of them so we can understand why some of the attitudes exist. *First, we have to face the fact that some employees were hired to fill certain basic jobs, with no intentions that they would ever be moved up in the organization.* They are minimum-skills people doing minimum-skills work, and they look like ideal people for the jobs to be done. But this isn't working out as well as it sounds, and these people—for various reasons—now expect to move up in the organization. Not only that, but there are internal and external pressures to see that these people do, in fact, move up. So the problem arises, how do you take minimum-skilled people who have never done the work expected of them at the higher level and move them into jobs requiring more skill than they have? The answer is simple enough to figure out, but not that easy to do: Train them!

This introduces another aspect of the problem. *Few people have had much experience in training low-skilled workers to do higher skilled work*, especially workers who weren't hired with any idea of going higher. This lack of teaching experience compounds the problem, because the first reaction is to train the people just as you train anyone else. When this is done, the workers don't always respond very well, and the supervisors start to say the job is hopeless and that "these people can't learn anything." Training low-skilled workers takes special talents, as we will see, and is different from training a person who has the background and the frame of mind quickly to go higher in the organization. Attitudes are different on *both* sides, the trainer and the trainee, neither seeing the situation as it really is, many times.

The trainees may think that they can learn anything, or nothing, and the trainers may think the trainees ought to learn anything that's thrown at them in any old way, or that the trainee can never learn anything no matter what kind of training is done. Any incorrect combination of these attitudes can be disastrous to the results. If the trainees don't think they can learn anything and the trainer thinks they can learn everything, the trainer is going to be discouraged about the same time the trainee is, which is very early. By the same token, if the learner doesn't realize the learning difficulties and the instructor thinks the learner is too stupid to learn anything, again we have a pretty sorry situation.

There is another aspect that should be taken into consideration. When organizations make a decision to move their people up, sometimes they do it with little regard to the workers' ability of suitability to do the job under consideration. If a job selection procedure is used, it may be poor. To make it worse, there may be an unwritten "quota system" implied that makes the supervisors believe that they must move up a certain number of people regardless of their qualifications. When we consider how carefully we normally hire people—specific people for specific jobs—and how carefully we normally promote people, we can easily see the difficulties that would arise if we just went out and moved anybody up without regard to any type of qualification. We've certainly reduced the possibilities of success in both the teaching and the learning. This doesn't mean that there can't be success; it just means that we've complicated the picture a lot and have made it harder for the employee being trained and the supervisor doing the training.

We'll have a chance to examine each of these aspects in more detail as we go along in this chapter, and we'll see that there are other problems that have to be overcome. We don't want to make the picture look too dreary, by the way. A number of things work in our favor, and we should be sure to use them as much as possible. For example, we know that quite often there are those who are just waiting to be "turned on." They are just waiting for a supervisor to give them a chance to learn something new, and when the opportunity shows up, they are ready to start with no need for motivation. These kinds of people make supervision a real pleasure, and it wouldn't be fair to say that they are rare. Most people are hoping to get an opportunity to move up, and most of them are willing to make the effort to get there. Supervisors sometimes get discouraged by the few that aren't interested in improving themselves and often let these people overshadow the better employees. Even those who are not necessarily excited about spending much of their own time in self-improvement will often perk up when someone else shows an interest in them. Many of these low-skilled people have had very little success at learning, and especially not at teaching themselves, so they aren't "self-starters" so far as learning is concerned. They may even lack confidence in their ability to learn since they've had very little success at it. This leads us to discuss the nature of many of the low-skilled people.

CHANGE OF ATTITUDE NEEDED

Remember, we're talking about those low-skilled people who haven't shown great excitement about learning. They aren't those who come to us and ask for a chance to learn, nor are they those who have scored well on entrance tests or who have been appraised as having a great attitude toward the job and the organization. These may be people who have shown themselves to be almost sullen or disinterested in the job. They aren't necessarily doing a bad job—just not burning up the track. They may not take to correction well, nor look as if they enjoy being told how to do something. In fact, it would be quite natural for us to classify them as having a "poor" attitude. It's nothing we can put our finger on—they're not what we'd call "ideal" employees. And therein lies our problem: *They don't act like the kind of employees we'd like to have.* They don't put out extra effort; they aren't eager to learn; they aren't down there after work trying to learn more; they don't ask a lot of questions; they don't rush out to put into practice what we'd just told them to do; they don't hang on to every word we say; they don't show an almost "reverent" attitude toward the organization, and particularly our own group. Because of the things they *don't* do, we consider them as having an attitude that is unacceptable for training toward a higher job. It's this kind of thinking that's made the job of training for upward mobility so difficult!

Our reasoning tells us that when employees aren't respond-ing as we expect *normal* employees to, then they don't "deserve" to be trained or moved upward. That used to be sound reason-ing, and for years that was the standard. We have to remember what we said earlier in this chapter about one of the aspects of the problem. It's all right to let the employees decide if they want to move up when we've hired *only* those people who are capable of moving up, or when we've hired a group of people who never expect to move up and know they will never get that chance and are satisfied to stay at their present level no matter who gets moved ahead of them. But we aren't in that situation now, as we have said already. Our "norm" has changed, and our *reasoning* needs to change with it. We can no longer deal with what an employee "deserves" and doesn't deserve. We have to think quite differently, and it makes sound reasoning, when we do think differently. For example, suppose we have an employee who is capable of moving up—even though this apti-tude stays well hidden. Suppose this employee doesn't get the chance, doesn't get the training. If there is a need for someone at that higher level, how do we fill the job? Do we go out and hire someone whom we will have to train, and then wait while the new employee acquires the experience and understanding to do the job? It would have been easier, cheaper, and quicker if we could have done a successful job of moving the existing em-ployee to this job, even if the training had taken more effort than usual and the employee had taken more time than usual to learn the job.

We now have to look at our attitude to see if maybe we haven't been making some false judgments about who gets trained and who doesn't. We finally come down to the question, "Does everyone deserve a chance to see if he or she has the capability of doing the job, or do we make the decision about certain people without ever training them or giving them the chance to show what they can do?" It's a difficult question to answer and has many ramifications. More and more, however, organizations are leaning toward the idea that everyone should get a chance to be trained—and that's a *fair* chance, meaning good training—regardless of their apparent attitude. It will take some time to get used to this idea, but for purely selfish reasons, if for no other, it pays off by giving us better employees for less money. In the end, we're finding that it also gives us employees with better morale and better attitudes. We'll see how as we go along in this chapter.

THE NEED FOR SUCCESS

Let's see what it takes to begin to get a response from lower skilled people. First, we have to understand that many of these people have never had much success at learning, so they aren't going to get too excited about it when we say we're going to train them. Next, we should realize that we haven't had too much success at training these kinds of low-skilled workers, either, so we will have to tread cautiously. What is needed is some obvious success on both our parts. The employee needs some success at learning, and we need some success at training. (They probably need it a lot more than we do, by the way, so we should really worry only about them and do pretty well.) The people we're used to training may have fared very well in the learning field. They have finished high school or college and are used to learning. They aren't threatened by the thought of learning something new as the low-skilled workers are. On the other hand, *the lower skilled worker often has so little success that even the smallest kind of learning may be a great threat*. Learning must take place in small doses and success must be frequent. The successes don't have to be very big, just not very far apart in the beginning. As the successes at learning come along, confidence will be built up, and the time between successes can be lengthened. This may sound ridiculous to us, but we aren't used to thinking about learning as being a threat, either. Our usual thought is that the more we learn, the better off we are. We're dealing with people who may think the opposite: The more they have to learn, the worse off they'll be. Not because the learning itself will be harmful, but because *having* to learn is such a chore.

Just what do we mean by "success"? Again, what success is to us and what success is to the underskilled may be quite different. We can work for a long time on a challenge, just because it's a challenge and we enjoy the struggle to solve the problem. We've done it before, and we have confidence we can do it again. That's because we've got the track record to prove it. But we're talking about people who have a pretty good track record, too: a record of *failure*. *Whatever challenges they've had so far as learning is concerned, they've nearly always lost.* They didn't get the highest grades in school, nor did they even get into the competition for these top grades. They didn't get satisfaction out of doing homework or taking tests because they got the wrong answers or no answers at all. While this is a little exaggerated, it's not a completely wrong picture. We're now in the situation where we are going to have to turn this thinking around. We can't do it overnight. We can't do it with one or two incidents. We can't make it permanent in a very short time. We can, however, make some great strides toward getting them to see that they *can* learn, and the kinds of successes we're talking about are easy and simple to give. When we're doing the training, we simply look for anything that's being done right and reward it with a compliment, a statement saying it's right, a nod of the head, an occasional pat on the back, even a public statement to our boss about the success the person is having. It's up to the trainer to pick out the successes and to acknowledge them. The rule of thumb is if we're a little in doubt as to whether to praise or "reward" the employee during the learning, do it anyway. Part of this rule is that it doesn't take big successes, just frequent ones.

A POSITIVE APPROACH

One more rule of thumb is to take a positive approach in our training effort. When we begin our training, we say to ourselves and to the individual, "There won't be any problems here." *"You can do it," should be our motto*, and we should really believe it. Part of the rule says that we don't just believe it ourselves, we set up a goal for the trainee. We determine in our mind that we aren't going to be satisfied until the *employee* believes that the learning can be done. We should not wait until the end of the training to see that this belief is there, either. We need to see it very early in the training effort. We need to see it *before* we get into much serious training. Let's see how it's actually done.

When we start the training , we approach the employee with a positive air about us. We certainly don't do as some have done and say something like, "Well, this is going to be pretty tough, so let's get at it," or "You may not get this the first time, but if you keep at it I think you'll understand it finally." That's not what we call a "positive" approach. We'd do better with, "Here's something you're going to enjoy," or "Since you've done so well on the other training, you surely won't have any trouble with this." This may sound a little "buttery," but we've got to say something to the employee, so it might as well be as positive as possible. Even a pleasant "Good morning" or "Good afternoon" is better than a sour or negative word. As we've mentioned earlier in the book, don't make the mistake of downgrading the training effort, either. Don't lead into it with a statement like, "We'd better hurry and get this over with so we can get back to something important," or "I hate to take up your time with this training, it shouldn't take but a few minutes." We should make it clear when we start the training that this is the most important thing we've got to do today and that much of the employee's future prospects depend upon getting as much training as possible.

Part of this positive approach includes making the early moments of the training very rewarding and successful. Good trainers see that the training is designed so that there is early accomplishment. Some of this can be simply a feedback session with the employee. Find some things that you are reasonably sure the employee knows and ask some questions about it. You should be certain that the employees know these things anyway, so asking them early will serve both as feedback to you and encouragement to the employees. The questions might be step-by-step procedures for doing the job, asked in the order the work is done. This will add some reinforcement to the job itself and allow the employee to get a little refresher course before the training starts. The questions shouldn't be tricky ones that will confuse the employee, but rather straightforward ones designed to lead the employee toward the answers.

PROCEDURES

Now let's see if we can put some of these "rules" together to come up with some effective training. We're working with an employee who may be in need of motivation. We've found one solution for that: success. Next, we've found the employee may not be very skilled at learning; also, we may not be very skilled at training this type of employee. So, again, we go to success as the key. We need some success ourselves—success in being able to train the employee to do something. Altogether this begins to give us a pattern of training. First we approach the assignment with an attitude of "this is going to be a success." We share this enthusiasm for success with the employee. Because we have done our planning well, we start off with some questions designed to give us and the employee some simple successes. We ask questions about the job that will give us feedback, give the employee a chance to answer some questions correctly, as well as give some success early in the training. Now comes the critical part.

When we get to the actual training on new procedures or activities, we need to be sure that we go about it in *small steps*. Many times we fail in our training efforts because we tend to break up the training into equal parts. This is poor training if we'll stop to think about it for a moment. The employee has to "taper on" to the learning, which means simply getting used to the learning, the new activity, the training itself. If we go about the training in small doses in the beginning, we allow the employee to avoid threats of not being able to learn. *Small steps with big successes* ought to be our goal in the early stages. As the successes continue, the steps can get longer. The threat level goes down with the number of successes. But this is just good training for *anyone*, not just the low-skilled. When we aren't in the habit of concentrated study, we do better if we start out gradually, then move on to bigger challenges.

In any kind of on-the-job training, the more steps we have, the easier it is to retain and to correct if we see something going wrong. The learners retain more because they don't have to remember such long, involved steps. We can do better at correcting because we don't have to wait so long to see the operation being performed, so we can see errors quickly and correct them just as quickly. Experience shows that with low-skilled employees, the duration of the training is an important consideration, too. While those employees who are used to learning and used to facing the challenge of new activities are able to go for longer periods at a time in the learning process, the ones who aren't used to these things can't go nearly as long. There is no set time limit, but the person doing the training has to be alert to the situation and recognize when they are beginning to lose interest. This may be after fifteen minutes or after an hour. It will vary with the job and the individual. It won't do any good just to say, "You'd better pay attention; you're going to need this!" If the attention span runs out, then the learning capability has run out too. *We're kidding ourselves if we think we can continue to train when the employee has tuned us out!*

FOLLOW-UP AND EVALUATION

We won't spend a lot of time here talking about evaluating the results of our training since we have a whole chapter on the subject, but there are a few things that need to be said about this as it relates to the low-skilled workers we've been talking about. We have tried to make the point that these people aren't hopeless, nor should we baby them in any way. They can and will go on to be some of our best employees, learning and progressing very well. Not all of them will, of course, but not all of our employees of any kind will go on and be those kinds of people. Just as we've suggested to you that *you* always take a positive attitude, *we'd* like to do the same thing. Again, we'd like to say that there is much evidence to show that *people usually become what we expect them to be*. They become what we think they are and what we tell them they are. If we think they are going to be slow learners and are always going to have a poor attitude, then that's just what we'll get in them. If we think they can learn and they will become loyal employees with good attitudes, then there's a very good chance that we'll get that kind of employee. Let's see how all of this fits into the evaluation process.

What are we evaluating? Actually, several things. First, we are evaluating the person doing the training. Perhaps this is the most important evaluation of all. Everything else depends upon how well this person did the training. It's not going to be fair to put a notation on the employee's record saying that there has been training when the training has been of poor quality or second rate. If the training has been excellent, then we can look at the results more openly. We can judge the employee much better if we know the training has been all right. (We aren't asking for perfection, of course, but the training shouldn't "get in the employee's way" of learning.) If we are going to evaluate the employee's progress based on training, we should make sure the employee gets the best possible training. How do we evaluate the trainer? Usually, that must be a self-evaluation process in on-the-job training, which puts a very heavy burden on the trainer to be unbiased. Honest introspection is perhaps one of the hardest things for a supervisor. We don't always see what's really there. We often see what we *want* to see, or what we think would be good to see, but often not what's really there. Perhaps more than anything else, though, we just don't look at ourselves at all when it comes to evaluation. If we're going to come up with objective evaluations of how the training has gone, we must have some idea of what we've done and what could have been done better. Only then are we in a position to decide how well the *employee* has done on the training. And that's the next thing we must evaluate: the employee.

We evaluate the trainee by performance, after we've decided that we've done our job well. We look at the employees we've trained and decide if they really are now able to do the job we want them to do. We ask the simple question: Is there a *deficiency*? In Chapter 1 we talked about deficiency as being the reason for doing the training. This is true even in training for upward mobility. We can think of the deficiency as anticipated, that is, a deficiency that would exist if the person were to try to do the job before training took place. If we've followed the things discussed in this book, we would not have done any training until we had determined just what that deficiency is and done training only on that area of performance. When it comes time to do the evaluation, we have only to look at the deficiency—or anticipated deficiency—to see how well the training has taken hold. If we haven't identified the deficiency ahead of time, there is little hope that we can do a very good job of evaluating our training.

We've talked about follow-up and evaluation. One element of evaluation is a direct tie-in with follow-up. The ultimate end of any training is the performance on the job. No matter how well the employee does in the training session or how well the employee likes the training or how good the attitude of the trainee is, if the employee can't perform on the job when it comes time to do the thing trained on, *then we can't say the training was satisfactory*. When we've decided what the employees are capable of doing and trained them in order to provide them with the capacity for upward mobility and they get the job that is in fact a step up the ladder—and the time comes for them to start to perform—that's when we need to do the follow-up on our training. That's when we want to know how well the training was done. There are several things that have to be taken into consideration, of course. The employee may or may not like the new job, hence may or may not want to perform well. The new supervisor may not like the idea of having this employee, so that may influence the performance. The others in the work group may have something to say about this employee working there, so that may influence behavior some. The degree to which we are perceptive is the degree to which we will be able to separate these influences and training deficiencies. We have to realize, as sad as it is, that we may try to find something like these things to blame if the training isn't doing its job. But we can also tell if the situation isn't conducive for the training to be converted into actual behavior. If we hear supervisors say that they don't expect to get much satisfactory work out of these newly promoted people, or that they don't think the organization is right in promoting them, or that it doesn't matter what kind of training they've had, "I always have to train them in my own way of doing things," then you can be sure that no matter how good the training was, it isn't going to work very well here. This is the third area of evaluation, then: the environment where the work will be taking place. It's a good idea to get some feel for it ahead of time, but that may not always be practicable. If not, then following up at the actual work site will be the next best thing.

TRAINING TECHNICAL AND HIGH-SKILLED EMPLOYEES

Most of what we've said so far has to do with training the lower skilled personnel, usually at the beginning or entry level. We need to spend a little time discussing the higher skilled people and their particular needs. It might be simpler just to suggest that we could take the opposite of what has been said and apply it here. We'll see that this is true in many cases.

For example, where many of the low-skilled workers are leery—sometimes fearful—of learning situations even when they want to learn, that is not so of the high-skilled employees. In this group we have people who have spent a lifetime to this point learning successfully. There needs to be no "change in attitude" about learning, unless it be that they may resent the mundane approach of learning step by step as we've seen in this book. For that reason, it is usually a good idea to explain to them why we are going through the various steps. Explain how much better people retain information and skills when they are involved in saying and doing, instead of just listening. (Remember, these people have gotten a great deal of what they know through listening to lectures or reading books. That's fine for these people learning things that fall in the category of facts or even specific knowledge of a job. However, when it comes to the psycho-motor skills, learning still takes the methods shown in this book. They may get bored with some of the steps, but preparing them with explanations will help.)

Changing Our Attitude

The real necessity of changing attitudes may be that we may need to change our attitude about these high-skilled, quick-learning people. We have to be sure that we don't resent them and their ability to learn. Like the low-skilled employees, they might not hang on to every word we say, but it may be because they're bored with what we say, wanting to get on with the actual hands-on portion of the training. For this reason, we need to exercise a willingness to test them and see if they're actually ready to move on instead of listening some more to us talk. They aren't used to waiting, especially when they think they already know something. This is a good place to get some involvement in order to get feedback on where they are in their learning process. Without being sarcastic, ask them how they understand something, or ask them to explain how to explain a process or procedure or the safety considerations . . . anything that will give us adequate feedback on just where they are.

The Need for Challenge

We found that low-skilled people needed frequent, small successes in order not to become intolerant of the learning experience. In the case of high-skilled people, it's a matter of getting plenty of challenge, but not necessarily frequently. They will work on a problem for hours or even days, just to get to the solution, whereas the lower skilled people aren't used to using patience in getting an answer. This doesn't mean that we make the jobs more complex or confusing; it just means that we shouldn't worry too much if what we're saying may require some time with a reference manual after the training is over. Learning may be a chore for the lower skilled employees, but it is a matter of accepted fact with the higher skilled people that learning must take place in order to do the job. (Actually, they may find that learning is a welcome relief from the boredom of the job.)

A word of caution here: The challenge should be in their need to go into more depth for reasons and implications, not to find hidden information that we've purposefully left out to make it hard for them. That's too much like playing games, and these people are too serious about learning to play games with us! What they are looking for more than anything else is the opportunity to learn how to do their jobs better, or how to do another, more challenging job. If we allow them to do that, they'll be eager and ready to learn from us any time we want to teach them something.

Still Stay Positive

We saw the need to be positive about the learning with low-skilled workers. We need to keep them pumped up about how easy it will be for them, and how quickly they will be able to learn the new skill. None of that means anything to the person who is used to having easy success at learning. It would be more of an insult than a matter of motivation. On the other hand, there is still a need for a positive approach, with us being positive about how much better this new method is than the old. Or, where these new skills will lead the employee, or even how much more valuable the employee will be to the company. We might even be positive about the satisfaction he will get from knowing how to do this new assignment.

We have an employee who is fairly well motivated, who doesn't need to be sold on how well he or she will be able to do, and who expects to succeed, not fail. We have employees who need challenge, not successes. What does that tell us? Where we had to do the training for the low-skilled people in small bits, being careful not to add any stress, we can stop worrying about that with these types of employees. We don't have to go for small steps, with careful, simple explanations. We won't have to do nearly as much repeating as we did with the other employees. We are dealing with workers who have a longer retention span, an interest in learning, and the ability to grasp what we say the first time we say it. It is always good to give commendations for good jobs, and this is no exception. We just don't have to make it sound like we're surprised that the learning took place!

Evaluation Is Still Needed

Just because the trainees are highly skilled and used to learning, it doesn't follow that we're infallible in our training skills. Hence, we still need to do a certain amount of follow-up on our training effort. We need to check to see if there are any questions, if the procedures are being followed, and if there is cognitive awareness of the things that were said, as well as things that were done. In other words, did we get it into the head as well as the hands? Here, again, we're evaluating ourselves as trainers, as much as evaluating the trainee as to his or her learning ability.

CONCLUSION

What have we said about training for career advancement? We've said that it is difficult because the trainee is often unskilled at learning, and the trainer is likely to be unskilled at handling the kind of training that's necessary for the low-skilled people usually involved in upward mobility training. We've said that the way to overcome some of the bad attitudes is to provide early and frequent successes during the training. We've said that we must exhibit a positive attitude before and during the training activity. Finally, we've suggested several things that need to be evaluated: the trainer, the training, the trainee, and the environment where the job is to be done, including the supervisor's attitude where the trainee will be working. All of this comes out to be worth it, however, since we end up with a well-trained employee, one that would have been wasted in a lower skilled job if we hadn't been concerned enough to provide some upward mobility training. The end easily justifies the means of getting there!

QUESTIONS FOR SMALL GROUP DISCUSSIONS

1. List at least three people in your own work group who could actually do a more skilled job if they were trained. (Make sure that you don't do this assignment lightly. If you say you don't think you have anybody, you should be willing to say that every person you supervise is right now, every day, working to top capacity and could never learn *another thing* about the job.)

2. Work up a training program—briefly outlining it—for one of the people you selected in Question 1. Choose one or two of the suggested programs to discuss in class. Discuss the feasibility of doing this training.

3. Break into subgroups and see if it's possible to put a price tag on the training it would take to bring people up one level on the job scale. Now compare this with the cost of hiring and training someone from the outside. See how the costs compare over the three people each person selected. Is there a money savings?

4. Without necessarily arriving at any conclusions, discuss the difference in attitude between a college graduate and a high-school dropout. Are these differences real? Does this mean that we should hire only college graduates? Does it mean we should hire only high-school dropouts?

5. Working in small groups, see which group can come up with the longest list of ways to offer "success" to the person who isn't used to getting much success in learning.

6. Record the lists from Question 5 on the board for everyone to see, then try to rank the suggestions as to the ease of using them and to their possible advantages or disadvantages.

EPILOGUE

Congratulations! Some reward should be offered if you have indeed reached this point. There are several things we can be sure of by now. Much of what you have read in this book was not new to you. Some of it you probably didn't agree with. Perhaps some of it was both interesting and helpful to you. The fact that you got this far indicates you have a desire to improve yourself both as a supervisor of people and as an instructor of people. But don't stop there. Try out what you have read about in this book. Use your own intelligence and think of things that were not written here—ways of improving your ability to teach others how to do their jobs. One of the best "motivators" for learning is *learning itself.* If you cause employees to learn, they will not only appreciate what they have learned, they will appreciate you as well. And it is appreciation well deserved.

appendix A

CHECKLISTS FOR SUPERVISORS

The following checklist gives the main areas where supervisors need to look in preparation for the training to be done. The supervisor should be able to check a "Yes" answer for each of the topics before going on with the training.

Personal Preparation Checklist

Action to be checked:	Yes	No
1. Is the supervisor *mentally* prepared for the training? (Is convinced that this is a training problem and that training will work; that this is the right time and the right training for the person on the job.)	___	
2. Is the supervisor *technically* prepared for the training? (Knows the job, not only the overall activity but enough of the step-by-step procedures to perform the training.)	___	___
3. Does the supervisor have a recent and accurate job analysis of this particular job? (Is aware of the steps in detail and with procedures approved by the organization.)	___	___
4. Has the supervisor provided for a training area for the training to take place? (Should provide for an area clear of people as much as possible, clear of distractions, and available for use for the length of time needed for the training.)	___	___
5. Does the supervisor have specific performance objectives available? (Knows what is expected of the employees when the training is over.)	___	___

Employee Preparation Checklist

Action to be checked:	Yes	No
1. Is the employee *mentally* prepared for the training? (Convinced that this training will offer a chance to improve on the job.)	___	___
2. Is the employee aware of personal deficiencies? (Knows specific areas of performance that aren't up to standard, and believes that this training, at this time, is going to address that deficiency.)	___	___
3. Is the employee able to understand and apply this training? (Has the experience, practice, and ability to learn this skill at this time.)	___	___
4. Does the employee know when the training will take place and about how long it will last? (Is aware that a time has been designated, as well as a place, and that the training is a planned activity not just something that is happening because there's nothing else to do.)	___	___
5. Does the employee know and understand what is expected after the training is over? (Realizes that there are some specific expectations of the training, and that these will be measured.)	___	___
6. Does the employee see the training as an opportunity? (Sees a chance to improve, not something designed for punishment.)	___	___

Training Location Checklist

Activity to be checked: Yes   No

1. Has the training place been checked for availability? (For full period of training requirements, including practice.)   ____   ____

2. Is the training location free of debris and raw materials? (So there is nothing in the way of the training and room for both the employee and the supervisor.)   ____   ____

3. Are the acoustics satisfactory in the training location? (Free from interfering noises from people and other equipment.)   ____   ____

4. Has the equipment itself been checked? (To be certain it is in working order and that all necessary tools, materials, and equipment are readily available.)   ____   ____

5. Do the people associated with the training location know that training is going to be taking place? (So there will be no talking or other interference with the training effort.)   ____   ____

6. Is the training location enough like the real environment to give a feel for reality? (Including looks, sounds, smells, etc.)   ____   ____

7. Is there an alternate location in case of a problem? (Such as equipment failure or need for the equipment by others of higher priority.)   ____   ____

appendix B

HOW TO DO ON-THE-JOB TRAINING

This appendix contains a suggested course for "How to Do On-the-Job training." There is a format for developing the OJT program, followed by the actual exercises that can be used for this format.

FORMAT FOR DEVELOPING A "TRAIN-THE-TRAINER" PROGRAM

I. **Purpose of the course:**
Train those who will be conducting on-the-job training programs, i.e., operators, supervisors, trainers, or anyone who needs to know how to train someone in a job (psycho-motor) skill.

II. **Objectives:**
A. Enable a trainer to go through a series of activities that will enable him or her to conduct on-the-job training in such a manner that there will be a reasonable guarantee that the trainee will be able to perform satisfactorily at the end of the training.

B. Enable the trainer to explain the importance of following the precise steps as revealed in the training program.

III. **Number of participants:**
The course is recommended for no more than twelve participants, in order to be able to monitor their activities. Ideally, there should always be an even number of people involved in the training, so they can always work in pairs.

IV. **Classroom arrangement:**
The best arrangement is to have the participants seated in a U-shape configuration, allowing the instructor to visit each work station from the opposite side (as opposed to a workbench against a wall).

V. **Length of the course:**
The course can be conducted in three to four hours, depending upon how many participants are involved. With eight people, three hours should be adequate; four hours would be needed for twelve people.

VI. **Equipment required:**
If specific tools or equipment are available, there should be enough for at least half of the participants. If no such

items are available, a satisfactory course can be taught with such items as staplers, 3-hole punches, mechanical pens, and other small office equipment.

VII. **Conducting the course:**
Step 1: Preparing the students. Following the information offered in this book, the students should be prepared for the training and given the set of objectives given in this outline.

Step 2: Introduction. Participants should be given information showing that while we *lose* about 80 percent of what we hear—without illustrations or without doing anything, our retention is about 90 percent when we describe what we are doing as we do it. They should then be given the steps in preparing for training, such as preparing the students, preparing ourselves to train, developing objectives, etc., following the points made in this book.

Step 3: How to do on-the-job training. The diagram showing the six steps to doing on-the-job training should be developed in the training room, and then the instructor should demonstrate for the participants. From that time on, the participants should be practicing.

VIII. **Student training:**
A. Participants should be paired off, then asked to designate one as an "A" and one as a "B". The As become the first trainers, the Bs become the trainees. Each pair is assigned a tool or a piece of equipment. Together they must first analyze the equipment, agree on names to call each part, and write a task analysis showing the step-by-step procedures for doing the task.

B. When both have agreed on the steps to operate the equipment, A should begin to train B, using the six steps. (The instructor should make an effort to monitor part of each training effort to be certain the steps are being followed.) When A is satisfied that B can perform the task properly, the roles should be reversed and B becomes the trainer.

C. After all have had an opportunity to be both the trainer and trainee, partners should be swapped so that no one is paired with the same person. Equipment is also switched so that no one is working on the same piece. The above procedures should be repeated.

D. The final activity is to have two pairs demonstrate before the class, allowing the class to become critiquing observers.

HOW TO DO ON-THE-JOB TRAINING

Exercise 1-A:

List below the reasons why any organization spends money, time, and person-hours on training:

Exercise 1-B:

List below reasons why employees would ever bother to spend the time, energy, and thought-power to learn:

Exercise 1-C:

List below reasons why people sometimes *don't* want to learn:

The Adult Learner:

1. List below the characteristics of adult learners and compare them to the child learner.

Adult Learner	*Child Learner*
1.	1.
2.	2.
3.	3.
4.	4.
5.	5.
6.	6.
7.	7.
8.	8.

2. All learners usually fall into one of three categories. List these categories below.

1.

2.

3.

Each person should pick one operation, preferably a small one, or a small part of a large one, for use during the entire train-the-trainer session. List the specific job, as described by the instructor, and save this page.

Job Analysis:

Complete the following chart for a simple activity, like sacking groceries, changing a tire (removing the lugs), lighting a cigarette, etc.

Step #	_Activity_
1.	
2.	
3.	
4.	
5.	
6.	
7.	
8.	
9.	
10.	
11.	
12.	
13.	
14.	
15.	

Goals/Objectives:

Pick three or four steps in the "Job Analysis" and complete the following chart, showing the "standards" as measurable, observable, or doable:

Step #	_Activity_	_Standard_

Content (Knowledge/Skills):

Pick the items you developed in "Objectives/Goals" and list all the knowledge and skills required to perform the task:

Objective   *Knowledge*   *Skill*

Motivation/Capability/Experience:

Consider the following and describe how you would approach and train each person:

1. Motivation high; capability high; experience high:

2. Motivation low; capability high; experience high:

3. Motivation high; capability high; experience low:

4. Motivation high; capability low; experience low:

5. Motivation low; capability low; experience high:

6. Motivation low; capability low; experience low:

7. Motivation high; capability low; experience high:

8. Motivation low; capability high; experience low:

In each case, consider the following:

1. *Preparing yourself*

2. *Preparing the employee*

3. How you would *begin*

4. How much *initiative* the employee would take

5. How much *follow-up* would be required

Doing the training:

On the task assigned by the instructor, write the steps to be taken, and what you would do in each case:

1.

2.

3.

4.

5.

6.

Now practice on each other until everyone has had a chance to train someone else.

INDEX